HOW
TO
Clean
YOUR
HOUSE

About the Author

Lynsey, Queen of Clean is one of the UK's most popular cleaning bloggers with over 100k Instagram followers and a blog reach of around 40/50k per month. Her devoted followers turn to her every day for her expert tips and tricks. Lynsey was first seen back in 2014 on Channel 4's *Obsessive Compulsive Cleaners* where she was a regular cast member cleaning some of Britain's dirtiest homes. She runs a successful cleaning company and regularly appears on UK shopping channels.

LYNSEY CROMBIE
QUEEN OF CLEAN

HOW TO *Clean* YOUR HOUSE

AND TIDY UP YOUR LIFE

ONE PLACE. MANY STORIES

HQ
An imprint of HarperCollins*Publishers* Ltd
1 London Bridge Street
London SE1 9GF

This hardback edition 2019

2
First published in Great Britain by
HQ, an imprint of HarperCollins*Publishers* Ltd 2019

ISBN: 978-0-00-834194-7

Text design and typeset by Rosamund Saunders

Printed and bound in Great Britain by
CPI Group (UK) Ltd, Croydon CR0 4YY

To my three amazing children, Mollie, Olivia and Jake, who have given me the strength to become the person I am today. I wouldn't be able to face life's challenges without you.

Contents

PART 3: STAYING ON TOP OF THE MESS

PART 4: DON'T PANIC!

Introduction

Why do I call myself 'The Queen of Clean'? Well, I've always had a huge obsession for cleaning, but when I joined the cast of Channel 4's *Obsessive Compulsive Cleaners* back in 2012, one of my lovely friends presented me with a bright pink apron emblazoned with the slogan 'Lynsey Queen of Clean' and it has stuck with me ever since.

To explain to you where my major obsession for cleaning began, let me take you back a little. When I was young, growing up in London, my mum was always cleaning. Whenever I visited either of my nans, I saw that they were doing exactly the same – cleaning was definitely in the blood! I used to help my mum around the house a lot and I honestly believe that this is a really good move to make when you have young children – it teaches them basic life skills and encourages them to look after their belongings.

When I was 21, I moved out of home with a boyfriend. I stuck a rota of cleaning tasks on the fridge door, which my friends used to laugh at, but I was so proud that my little flat was super clean and organised. The skills I had learned when I was growing up certainly helped.

Jumping ahead a few years, tragedy hit me. I was married, living in Newcastle and pregnant with twins. I thought I had married a man who would offer me the world, but shortly into the marriage I made a terrible discovery about him and the shock sent me into labour, resulting in my twin daughters being born extremely prematurely. With no specialist facilities available in Newcastle, the girls were flown up to a special care baby unit in Edinburgh, where I found myself alone with two very poorly babies after my world had been completely turned upside down. I don't want to go into more detail here but I have discussed this previously on my blog if you're interested to hear more about my story.

The connection with my ex-husband sent me into cleaning over-drive. I scrubbed and scrubbed everything in sight to wash away the pain that my husband had caused me. In addition to this, special care baby units are very sterile places – you are encouraged to constantly wash your hands before you touch your babies. This situation added fuel to the fire of my cleaning obsession.

After six weeks in special care, the stronger of my girls, Olivia, was allowed to come home. A few weeks later, Mollie came home too. Mollie needed an oxygen supply, so in addition to installing a home supply, I had to take a canister with us if we left the house. It was a really hard time; my babies were so small they had to be propped up in their pram with lots of towels and I remember people staring at us whenever we went out and about. I was very lonely living in Newcastle and I hadn't yet told my family and friends what I was going through.

Feeling very isolated and lonely, my daily walk would be to the local shops to buy cleaning products. Every day, I would load up the bottom of the pushchair with random cleaning products, then I would come home and obsessively clean until all the products were gone. This wasn't normal behaviour, but it was something that I could channel my anger and negative energy into. It also gave me an excuse to get out of the house for an hour or so.

Eventually, I found the courage to tell people back home what had happened. Swiftly, my dad turned up with a big white van, we loaded everything we could into it and I came back home. I felt that I was literally coming away with nothing: my children were poorly, I had no career and my marriage was over.

I felt ashamed at first, but after a few weeks at my parents' house, my dad found me a nice flat to rent. I loved my little flat – I kept it pristine and every day was very much regimented. Feeding twins isn't easy when you're on your own; everything has to be structured into a set routine that repeats itself daily. In between managing the twins, I fitted in a daily walk and a lot of cleaning to keep my mind busy. My little routine kept me in control and I really enjoyed being on my own with the girls. Being so structured helped my confidence start to grow again.

After a while, my health visitor helped me get a job as a receptionist in a local doctor's surgery. With the girls in and out of hospital, I spent so much time with medical teams that it felt rather fitting. This is where I met my new partner Rob – he was a medical rep and used to come into the surgery. It wasn't easy meeting someone new, as I had no trust at all. I had Rob CRB checked and used to watch every move he made with the girls by peering around door frames. I was a very angry person and I'm surprised he stuck around. I got better as time went on and realised he was a good role model for my girls. Two years into our relationship, I fell unexpectedly pregnant. It was a shock to the system, but having my son Jake really cemented us as a family and helped me get back on track.

As time went on, I grew stronger and started to get my confidence back. After Jake's birth, I found I was getting bored at home, so

I got some work in a local shelter for the elderly, helping them with their shopping, ironing and cleaning. The twins were now at school, so I would take 4-month-old Jake with me and he would just sleep in his car seat in the corner of the room. I loved the job. The older people looked forward to me coming and I looked forward to seeing them and I enjoyed hearing their stories. One old lady in particular also had a passion for cleaning and she used to show me her tips and tricks using all sorts of kitchen-cupboard products. I'll never forget the first time I tried putting bicarbonate of soda down the plug hole. I was mesmerised and completely fascinated. This is when I decided that I wanted to continue with my cleaning and help people.

It was the start of my cleaning journey. My little business was growing and I had a good bank of customers. I kept myself busy and I loved to make other people's houses shine. I really have had some amazing customers over the years. There are great benefits to cleaning for other people: you know you are making a difference to people's lives; you are earning a good honest living; and you are even keeping fit.

OBSESSIVE COMPULSIVE CLEANERS

I literally fell into the *Obsessive Compulsive Cleaners* TV show. I had watched the first series and absolutely loved it, but I would never have applied to be on the show. As well as cleaning, I used to work for a local magazine selling advertising space. One day, the production company called to place an advert as they were looking for people in the area with a NOT so clean home. I got chatting away to the person who had called and, before I knew it, there was full camera crew in my home auditioning me for the show! I was nervous, but also excited. I got the part instantly and, within a few weeks, I was heading up to Blackpool to film my very first episode.

Now, I didn't really believe a house could be as dirty as the ones I had seen in Series One. I also thought that I wouldn't actually be doing much cleaning and that a team of cleaners would be supporting me behind the scenes. I was so wrong. It was just me and the house was horrific! What had I got myself into?

It was exhausting but fun – I had an absolute blast. On one occasion I was quite naughty and, every time the homeowners weren't looking, I chucked a load of their stuff into the skip, which probably contributed to it becoming one of the most-watched episodes. As a result, the production company asked me to continue being part of the show.

I cleaned quite a few houses in the end and we even went out and about swabbing things like cash machines and people's pushchairs. The results were quite shocking. I also got to clean some fascinating old country manors, which were beautiful buildings that had become run down over the years. One of my favourite moments (which at the time was really painful, although I can now look back and laugh) was when I walked over a bedroom rug and fell right through the floor beneath it!

It was very challenging to chuck antique chairs with three legs into a skip only to see the home owners pull them back out again as they didn't want to part with their broken belongings. I found it really sad, but I was there to do a job and make their homes liveable again. I learned so much about the history of the houses and met some fascinating people.

Although the show has now come to an end, during my time on it I started to use Twitter and engage with a few brands. I was sent a few freebies, which was amazing, and I did start to get recognised when I was out and about.

SOCIAL MEDIA SUCCESS

My daughters joined Instagram when they hit Year 6 – apparently everyone at school was on it, so they had to be part of it too. I gave in and let them join, but under the condition that I could see everything they were posting and I set myself up with my own page: Lynsey_queenofclean. I kept an eye on the girls, but soon started to find some great fashion accounts. I got sucked in pretty quickly – I loved looking at the outfits these girls were putting together. I also started to follow a few home interior accounts, mainly because we had recently moved and I needed a little inspiration.

One day in 2016, I casually posted a picture of a bottle of cleaning product and added in a few hashtags (I'd learned how important the hashtags were from my girls and the fashion accounts I was following).

Within seconds I got loads of 'likes'. I only had about 40 followers, so where were all these 'likes' coming from? I thought it was madness that people liked my picture.

Over the next few weeks, I started posting random pictures of myself cleaning. The likes continued and I was gaining followers. I didn't know any of these people, so I found it quite strange at first, but I slowly started to piece together how Instagram worked. I did quite a bit of research and saw that this was a growing trend, that people were using Instagram to connect with those with similar interests, and that you could make money with an attached blog, too. When I hit around 10k followers and my blog was up and running, brands started to contact me and offer me free products. I was over the moon. I mean, for a girl like me, free cleaning products are absolute heaven!

Now I use Instagram and my blog to feature products and some of my little tips and tricks. I also give product demos – these have proved to be very valuable as they save people hunting for reviews online. I like to show people that cleaning isn't boring and can be really fun. I also talk openly about my past and how I used cleaning to save myself, which has been something my audience has really related to. I take the time to engage and interact with my followers and to support them. I encourage people to grab that mop daily, to get up off the sofa and do something positive, which in turn really does help support mental health.

I feel so proud to have created a community of people who have found comfort in cleaning. My social media journey has connected me with some amazing people and brought you this book. I hope you enjoy it as much as I have enjoyed putting it together for you.

 Happy Cleaning!

LYNSEY QUEEN OF CLEAN

BACK TO BASICS

The Perfect Cleaning Caddy

How to create your own Queen of Clean tool kit!

I am often asked by newlyweds, people leaving home for the first time and new home owners about the best cleaning tools and products. I know that, for some, this can be very confusing; the supermarket shelves are packed with so many products, it's hard to know what to buy.

My advice is to create a home cleaning kit. A perfectly-formed kit is the key to successful cleaning and will save you both time and money; you really don't need to have cupboards bursting with products. The other beauty of having a dedicated kit is that you have everything to hand and you will know when you are starting to run low and need to replenish items.

This section will help you put together the ultimate cleaning caddy that is not only practical, but well organised and transportable, and which contains all the essential cleaning products you need to keep your home clean and give you fantastic results.

When building your kit, consider creating a few smaller additional kits that you can keep in different places in your home. This will help save you time when you are cleaning, so that you don't have to go up and down the stairs like a yo-yo if you have forgotten anything.

Let's get started ...

You will need:

a sturdy, good-sized cleaning caddy with a handle

NATURAL CLEANERS

I tend to lean towards homemade products, so these few items are key if you are keen to follow the homemade, natural route.

+ White wine vinegar (a degreaser and a mild disinfectant)
+ Bicarbonate of soda (a natural mild abrasive and deodoriser)
+ Baby oil (great for shining-up stainless steel)
+ Essential oils (for fragrance)

BOUGHT CLEANING PRODUCTS

+ Multipurpose cleaner
+ Furniture polish
+ Washing-up liquid
+ Glass and mirror cleaner
+ Limescale remover
+ Bleach

CLEANING TOOLS

+ Rubber gloves
+ Sponges
+ Microfibre cloths (in a good mix of colours – see page 24)
+ Toothbrush
+ Wire wool
+ Lint roller
+ Squeegee
+ Duster

ADDITIONAL MUST-HAVE TOOLS

These obviously won't fit in your caddy, but you need them.

+ Vacuum
+ Mop and bucket

STORAGE

When choosing your caddy and products, think about where you are going to store them. Do you have a large enough space? It is so important to consider this before you go out and buy loads of items.

It's good to designate a space under your kitchen or bathroom sink or in your laundry room for cleaning products. Under-sink storage solutions are a great use of space and will free up other areas of your home.

If space is tight, don't panic – there are some great options available these days. Consider using over-the-door storage solutions. If you are using a mop and bucket, use the bucket for storing items. Roll up your cloths for easy storage, too.

Vacuums aren't always the easiest items to store and can take up valuable room. If cupboard space is limited, you could store your vacuum under your bed, in an under-stair cupboard, behind the sofa or even on top of the wardrobe, if it will lie flat.

Queen of Clean's homemade cleaner recipes

I am a huge fan of natural cleaning and making my own cleaning products. The air quality inside many homes can be two to five times more polluted than the air just outside. Traditional shop-bought household products play a huge part in creating this pollution, which is why I avoid them as much as I can. Besides, making your own products can be fun and most of the ingredients can be found in your own kitchen.

It's important to remember that homemade cleaning products don't last indefinitely – they only have a life span of around 3 months. Make small batches and replace them frequently. If you are using fresh lemon juice, you will only get one use from the cleaning solution, as the lemon juice will go off and not be effective thereafter.

Try to use smaller bottles when mixing your own products. I love to use 500 ml bottles – this size will give me enough product to last for a few weeks.

BENEFITS OF MAKING
YOUR OWN PRODUCTS

+ You control the ingredients.
+ They are cost effective (especially if you buy the ingredients in bulk).
+ Fewer chemical toxins means safe cleaning (particularly if you have pets or children).
+ Improved air quality.
+ Reduced probability of triggering asthma and allergies.

You will need:

+ Spray bottles (these can be recycled from existing store-bought products. Simply remove the labels, wash them out well and allow to dry)
+ Adhesive labels
+ Water
+ Lemons
+ Bicarbonate of soda
+ White wine vinegar
+ Soda crystals
+ Essential oils

TIPS FOR HOMEMADE PRODUCTS

+ Use 500 ml spray bottles for your homemade products.
+ Label all products clearly.
+ Use single-use products immediately and discard any product left over.
+ Other products will keep for a few weeks, but discard after 3 months.

ALL-PURPOSE CLEANER

Mix 120 ml/½ cup white wine vinegar and 50 g/¼ cup bicarbonate of soda into 2 litres/8 cups water. Mix until completely dissolved. Decant into a labelled spray bottle.

Use this solution for the removal of water marks on shower panels and bathroom chrome fixtures, and to clean windows and mirrors. Spray directly onto surfaces and wipe with a damp microfibre cloth.

WOODEN FURNITURE POLISH

I am often asked about how to clean real wood surfaces. Some of the products on the market are just far too abrasive and can take the colour out of the wood or damage fine polished surfaces. Using a natural cleaner will ensure your wooden surfaces are well looked after.

This simple, quick and easy polish won't cause any damage at all. Simply fill an empty spray bottle with 4 teaspoons olive oil, 4 teaspoons white wine vinegar and 10 drops of lemon essential oil and shake really well. A few sprays and a rub with a soft microfibre cloth and… voila! You will be left with the perfect finish.

NOTE: this polish is single use. Do all your woodwork on the same day to get full use of the solution.

AIR FRESHENERS

Air fresheners are commonly used to mask bad smells within the home, however they don't actually get rid of the smell altogether. Many of my natural solutions will absorb and remove the nasty odours for fresher, healthier air.

+ Dot bowls of fragrant dried herbs and flowers around the house.
+ A mixture of bicarbonate of soda or white wine vinegar with a hint of lemon juice placed in small dishes around the house will absorb unpleasant odours.
+ Put 3 teaspoons bicarbonate of soda and 8 drops of your favourite essential oil into a spray bottle and top up with water for a homemade deodorising spray.

- ✦ House plants help to reduce odours in the home.
- ✦ Prevent cooking odours by simmering 1 tablespoon vinegar in 1 cup water on the stove while cooking. Alternatively, simmer some cinnamon or other aromatic spices.
- ✦ To remove particularly pungent smells like fish and onions from utensils and cutting boards, wipe them over with vinegar, then wash them in soapy water.
- ✦ A halved onion left in the corner of a room will help absorb odours quickly.
- ✦ Keep fresh coffee grounds on your kitchen worktop.
- ✦ Freshen up your kitchen bin by dropping in slices of lemon.

FABRIC REFRESHER

You can make your own fabric spray to refresh your sofas, carpets, curtains and other fabric surfaces. Half-fill a spray bottle with boiling water, add 2 teaspoons bicarbonate of soda and a few drops of your favourite essential oil, shake to mix and leave for about 30 minutes for the mixture to infuse. Always spray items from a distance of at least 20 cm/8 inches and be careful around pets and children.

CARPET REFRESHER

For the freshest carpet, add 15 drops of your favourite essential oil to 200 g/1 cup bicarbonate of soda. Using a sieve, liberally sprinkle the mixture all over your carpet or rug, leave for a few hours, then vacuum it up.

This is one of my favourite tips; I do it myself once a week!

CARPET STAIN REMOVER

Mix equal parts white wine vinegar and water in a spray bottle. Spray directly onto the stain, let sit for several minutes, then clean with a brush or sponge using warm soapy water.

For fresh grease spots, sprinkle cornstarch (cornflour) onto the spot and leave for 15–30 minutes before vacuuming.

For a heavy-duty carpet cleaner, mix together 50 g/¼ cup salt, 50 g/¼ cup soda crystals and 60 ml/¼ cup white wine vinegar. Mix into a paste then rub into the carpet stain and leave it for a few hours. Vacuum it off.

DRAIN CLEANER

This is something I recommend you do weekly to prevent nasty odours and blockages.

Pour 100 g/½ cup bicarbonate of soda into the drain, then add 120 ml/½ cup white wine vinegar and leave for 15 minutes. The chemical reaction will help to break down fatty clogs. Flush with boiling water from the kettle.

Caution: Plastic pipes can be damaged if excessive boiling water is used. If you don't have metal plumbing, use warm or even cold water to rinse instead.

DISINFECTANT

Fill a spray bottle with 2 teaspoons soda crystals and 4 tablespoons white wine vinegar, then top up with hot tap water. Spray directly onto surfaces and wipe off with a damp microfibre cloth for powerful cleaning.

CROCKERY STAIN REMOVER

Remove coffee and tea stains from cups and mugs by adding 1 heaped teaspoon bicarbonate of soda to each, then filling with boiling water. Leave for about 30 minutes, then drain and rinse. You'll be amazed by the results!

CHOPPING BOARD CLEANER

Rub a slice of lemon over wooden or plastic chopping boards to disinfect the surface.

For tougher stains, squeeze some lemon juice directly onto the stain and scrub in a little salt. Leave for 10 minutes, then rinse clean.

CERAMIC OR GLASS HOB CLEANER

To save your hob becoming a sticky mess, make a point of cleaning it after every use. To remove stuck-on food, wet the area with hot soapy water and sprinkle with bicarbonate of soda. Cover with a damp towel or kitchen paper and leave for 30 minutes, then wipe with a clean damp cloth.

Microfibre cloths

I use a lot of microfibre cloths; I love how easy they are to clean with. Microfibre is a blend of polyester and polyamide (nylon) and each fibre is up to 50 times finer than a human hair. Ideal for high powered cleaning, the fine hairs in a microfibre cloth pick up and trap more dirt than standard cloths. General purpose microfibre cloths also have a small electrostatic charge, which makes them very effective for picking up dust.

Microfibre cloths can be used for almost any cleaning job and work particularly well if you clean with the 'S' action. Making an 'S' shape with the cloth means that you more effectively cover the entirety of the surfaces you are cleaning.

Dusting
Used both damp and dry, microfibre cloths make ideal dusters.

Electronics and glassware
Microfibre cloths are particularly good for cleaning electronics and glassware, including television and computer screens and tablets. As microfibre cloths don't pick up debris, they will not leave scratch marks.

Stainless steel
With just water and vinegar and using the 'S' action, microfibre cloths are great for giving stainless steel a shiny finish.

Chrome

When cleaning your chrome taps, use a microfibre cloth dipped in a solution of vinegar and water. This will remove any water marks, ground-in grime, and soap scum, leaving your taps beautifully shiny.

Eyewear

To clean glasses, rub them really well with a little rubbing alcohol on your microfibre cloth.

Grout and tiles

Grout can be very hard to keep clean and bright white. After scrubbing grout with a small hard brush or a toothbrush, use a microfibre cloth to wipe away any soapy suds and buff the grout and tiles clean and dry, leaving them super shiny.

Washing up

Another great tip is to use your microfibre cloths for the washing up. Microfibre cloths don't cling onto bacteria, so they don't end up smelling. When you're finished, make sure to wring out as much water as possible and hang up to dry.

Drying dishes

Microfibre cloths soak up water really well so are also great for drying the dishes. Use a separate cloth for drying after you've finished washing up.

Top tips to keep your microfibre cloths working for you longer

COLOUR-CODING CLOTHS

When cleaning your home, it's important to clean away the germs, not spread them around. Please don't use the same cloth for multiple household tasks. Imagine using the same cloth for the loo and the bath! Yuck! Try using a colour coding system for your microfibre cloths – this will stop cross-contamination of dirt and bacteria around the home.
Here's my system:

PINK for the SINK
BLUE for the LOO
GREEN for CLEAN
YELLOW for DUSTING

I use pink cloths for cleaning sinks, draining areas and work surfaces in the kitchen. In the bathroom, I use pink to clean the bath, shower and sinks.
Blue is for the toilet and only the toilet.
Green is actually for cleaning glass: mirrors, picture frames, windows, TV screens and glass-topped furniture (Green for Clean just sounds better!).
I use yellow for general dusting: furniture, skirting boards and banisters.

You can of course create your own system – just make sure it works for you!

WASHING

+ Wash your microfibre cloths between uses.
+ You may also want to wash the cloths before using them for the first time to remove any stray fibres.
+ You can either wash cloths by hand or in a washing machine. If you opt to use the machine, try to wash them separately from any other laundry.
+ Make sure to dry cloths out before you leave them in a laundry bin, as wet cloths will encourage mildew and bacteria growth.

Machine washing

Pop them in the washing machine at 60°C, with liquid detergent but no fabric conditioner and they will come out as good as new! I opt for liquid detergent over powder as powder can sometimes damage the delicate cloth fibres.

Hand washing

Wash with warm soapy water, adding in some washing detergent or even washing-up liquid. Leave to soak for about 1 hour and occasionally stir around with a wooden spoon. Rinse under cold running water.

Drying

One of the great things about microfibre cloths is how quickly they dry! All you need to do is hang them up to air dry. If you want to dry them in a tumble dryer, use a low heat as a high heat can damage and shrink microfibre cloths.

Tried and tested cleaning methods

USING VINEGAR

White wine vinegar is a godsend when it comes to cleaning. A weak form of acetic acid, it is effective at killing mould, bacteria and germs. In fact, every kitchen and bathroom will benefit hugely from a handy spray bottle containing a 50:50 solution of water and vinegar. Armed with just vinegar, here's what you can achieve:

IN THE KITCHEN ...

Descaling the kettle

I do this monthly and this trick has never let me down. Simply fill the kettle with half water and half vinegar and leave for 30 minutes. Once the time is up, boil the kettle then empty and rinse thoroughly. This will keep limescale at bay and eliminates the need for harsh chemicals. *You can also try this trick on your coffee machine!*

Remove kitchen sink odours

This is a task that you need to add to your monthly cleaning schedule. When combined with bicarbonate of soda, white wine vinegar can get rid of those nasty sink odours and keep your drain free of slime and gunk. See page 20 for my formula for a homemade drain cleaner. The mixture will break down fat and food residues, leaving your pipes blockage free and your drains smelling fresh. Afterwards, make sure you rinse well with freshly boiled water (if you have plastic pipes, rinse with cold or warm water). It takes no time at all and makes all the difference.

Clean and deodorise your microwave

Fill a microwave-safe bowl with 120 ml/½ cup vinegar and 250 ml/1 cup water, place in the microwave and put on a high heat for 5 minutes. Leave it in the microwave while it cools. Afterwards, you can easily wipe down the inside of the microwave and, as if by magic, those nasty odours will have miraculously disappeared!

Cleaning the fridge

Mix 4 teaspoons vinegar into a half-filled washing-up bowl of warm water and use the solution to wipe down your refrigerator's interior, including the shelves, walls and even food packaging, if necessary. Your fridge will be clean and fresh-smelling without the need for harsh chemicals that could contaminate food.

Wash fruit and veg

Vinegar helps remove bacteria and pesticide residues from fruit and vegetables. Mix 3 parts water to 1 part white wine vinegar, and dispense in a spray bottle. Rinse clean.

Getting rid of kitchen smells

Add a mixture of water and vinegar to a saucepan and boil on the hob for 15 minutes to get rid of any nasty odours in your kitchen. This is particularly good after cooking.

Shine drinking glasses

A great pre-dinner-party tip to remove marks from your glasses is to submerge them in a mixture of water and vinegar. Remove and leave to dry naturally, then wash again.

IN THE BATHROOM . . .

Limescale and hard water build-up

Limescale and hard water stains can be a real pain to remove and many of the cleaning products on the market just don't cut it. Vinegar is the solution. To achieve the perfect shine and remove any blockages from shower heads, fill a small plastic bag with vinegar, place it over the shower head and tie the bag securely at the top. A hand-held shower head can be submerged in a bowl of vinegar, if preferred. Leave it for a few hours then remove, rinse with water and wipe down. It really is that easy.

You can also spray neat vinegar onto shower doors, draining boards and taps. Just leave it for a few hours so it can work its magic before wiping it off.

Mould and mildew prevention

If you have any mould and mildew in the bathroom or on your shower curtain, spray with neat vinegar, leave for an hour or so, then rinse.

Toothbrushes

Soak your toothbrush heads in a mixture of vinegar and hot water to give them a good clean. Don't forget to rinse them thoroughly before using!

AROUND THE HOUSE ...

Window and glass cleaning

Spray a 50:50 solution of water and vinegar onto windows, mirrors and shower screens and wipe clean with a microfibre cleaning cloth.

Carpet stains

We've all been there, particularly if you have children. Vinegar can really help remove unwanted marks. Simply apply neat to the stain and leave it to work for about 15 minutes, then blot the stain with a white cloth or paper towel (this way, you can actually see if the stain is lifting). Repeat the process, if necessary, then rinse using a wet cloth with a little washing-up liquid.

Freshen up laundry

Add 1 capful vinegar to the machine if you feel your laundry is looking a little dull (use the same cap you use for dispensing your detergent). Your colours will come out bolder and your whites whiter.

Remove grass stains

Combine 80 ml/⅓ cup white wine vinegar with 160 ml/⅔ cup water. Apply the solution to the stain and blot with a clean cloth. Repeat this process until you've removed as much of the stain as possible, then wash as usual.

Cleaning your washing machine

Add 2 capfuls vinegar into the detergent compartment and run an empty hot cycle to freshen up your machine (use the same cap you use for dispensing your detergent).

USING LEMONS

I love having a bowlful of lemons in my house; not only do they help brighten up the kitchen but they can be really handy when it comes to cleaning. They smell gorgeous and will add that much needed sparkle and shine to your home. Here are some simple cleaning hacks to put those lemons to use:

HANDY HINT

You can also use the bottled pre-squeezed lemon juice that you can find in the cookery aisle in supermarkets.

IN THE KITCHEN . . .

Cleaning wooden chopping boards

You can clean your wooden chopping board with half a lemon and a little coarse salt. Sprinkle the salt over the chopping board, then use the cut face of the lemon to scour the surface of the chopping board, squeezing slightly to release the lemon juice as you go. Let it stand for about 15 minutes to give the lemon and salt some time to work, then scrape away the lemon and rinse with warm water and a clean sponge or cloth.

Limescale removal

Lemon is great at tackling limescale. For taps, simply cut a lemon in half and run the cut face all over the tap, wherever the limescale is present. Leave it for 15 minutes, so that the lemon juice can get to work, then rinse away. You may need to repeat the process.

To descale the kettle, just pop a few lemon halves (if you have used them already for juicing, this is OK, too) into the kettle, fill with water and boil. Leave overnight. In the morning, boil again before emptying, then give it a quick rinse to remove any bits.

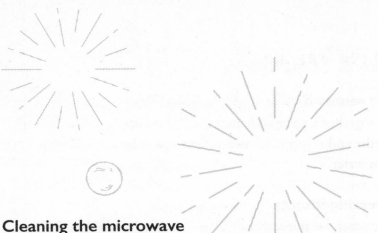

Cleaning the microwave

Put a few lemon halves into a microwave-safe bowl of clean cold water, pop it into the microwave and then put it on full power for 5 minutes. The lemon will break down any grease stuck to the sides, making it really easy to wipe off with a cloth afterwards.

Removing hard water marks

Hard water marks can be a real pain, but simply rubbing the mark with a halved lemon is an easy way to remove them. This is great for shower screens and draining boards.

Deodorising the fridge

Soak a clean sponge in lemon juice, put it on a saucer or in an open tub and leave in the fridge overnight. By the morning, your fridge will smell lovely and zesty fresh.

Dishwasher cleaning

Pour lemon juice into the sealed tablet section and then run on an empty hot wash.

Chrome polishing

Rub a halved lemon over taps to give them the ultimate shine.

AROUND THE HOUSE ...

Rust removal

Mix together a paste of lemon juice and salt. Apply this paste to the rust and scrub it in. Leave for a few minutes and rinse with warm water.

Deterring insects

In summer, keep insects out of the kitchen by squirting a drop of lemon juice wherever they usually enter the room.

Tackling laundry stains

Apply a mixture of lemon juice and salt to the stain and leave for 30 minutes, before rinsing and washing as normal.

Removing perspiration marks

To remove sweat stains from clothing, rub the area with a mixture of lemon juice and white wine vinegar and leave to work for 15 minutes. Rinse, then wash as usual.

USING BICARBONATE OF SODA

Newsflash! Bicarbonate of soda isn't just for making chocolate chip cookies but can be used for a whole host of household cleaning tasks. Bicarb has the power to freshen and clean your home to a dazzling shine. It's super effective, gentle and non-abrasive and is a great natural deodoriser. Here are my top household tips for cleaning with bicarbonate of soda:

IN THE KITCHEN ...

Refresh the fridge
One of the best uses of bicarb is to leave a small dish of it at the back of your fridge. This will soak up any nasty food smells and leave your fridge smelling zingingly fresh.

Scrub down kitchen surfaces
Nearly every grubby spot in your kitchen can benefit from bicarb – simply mix it with water to clean work surfaces, stainless steel sinks, microwaves, cooker hoods and cooking utensils.

Tupperware stains
Sometimes, leftover food stored in tupperware containers can leave nasty stains. Sprinkle stained containers with a layer of bicarbonate of soda, add a little warm water and leave for 30 minutes before rinsing. The bicarb will lift the stain, leaving your tupperware clean and sparkling.

Cleaning fruit and veg
Mixed with water, bicarb can remove the waxy coating on super-market-bought fruit and veg and remove any traces of dirt. Just remember to rinse before eating.

Bin odours
Sprinkle some bicarb into your bin to help keep food odours at bay.

Greasy dishes and pans
Tackle baked-on food by mixing bicarb with washing-up liquid and hot water. Use a sponge and you will find that the grease easily comes away.

Oven cleaning
Mix bicarb and water into a paste, then use it to cover as much of the oven interior as you can. Next, take a spray bottle containing a 50:50 mixture of water and white wine vinegar and spray over an even layer. Leave for at least 30 minutes, then rinse with warm water. You will find that the grease and grime lifts away without the need for any harmful toxins.

IN THE BATHROOM ...

Fighting mildew
Regularly scrub your bath, tiles and sink basins with bicarb, warm water and a sponge to keep mould and mildew away. For established mould and mildew patches, apply neat, leave for 1 hour, then rinse off to reclaim your bathroom.

Clearing bathroom and kitchen drains
Clear a stubborn blocked drain by pouring 100 g/½ cup bicarbonate of soda down it, followed by 120 ml/½ cup white wine vinegar. Leave for about 15 minutes, then flush with boiling water from the kettle. If you have plastic pipes just use warm water.

Grout cleaning
Mix bicarb and white wine vinegar into a paste and apply directly to the grout between floor or wall tiles with a small brush (a toothbrush works well). Leave for at least 30 minutes, then rinse. Your grout will come back to life and look as good as new.

AROUND THE HOUSE ...

Freshen pet beds
Sprinkle your pet's bed with bicarb, leave it for 15 minutes and then vacuum it off.

Crayon marks on walls
When your kid's artistic efforts end up all over the wall you just repainted, lightly scrub the marks with a damp sponge sprinkled with bicarb to remove.

Brighten your laundry whites
Add 1 heaped teaspoon bicarb to your washing detergent to bring your whites back to life.

Brighten dull-looking jewellery
When your silver stops shining, make a paste of 3 parts bicarbonate of soda to 1 part water, apply with a microfibre cloth (not a paper towel, which can scratch) and rinse.

Freshen trainers
Sprinkle those smelly trainers with bicarb and leave for a few hours for the bicarb to soak up the odours. Knock out the next day or vacuum out using the nozzle attachment.

Messy barbecue

Combat a summer's worth of cooking grime by sprinkling some bicarbonate of soda onto the grill-cleaning brush before scrubbing away.

Oil spills

Cover the spillage with bicarb, then scrub with a wet brush or broom to make it disappear.

Freshen kids soft toys

Place the toys into a large plastic bag and add a good sprinkle of bicarb. Secure the top, take the bag outside and shake well. The baking soda helps to draw out nasty smells and dust. Remove the toys from the bag and vacuum the bicarb away.

Upholstery

Banish smells from your sofas, chairs and mattresses and give them a really good refresh by sprinkling evenly with bicarb (I suggest using a sieve). You can also add in a drop of your favourite essential oil, if wished. Leave for 15 minutes before vacuuming it off.

USING TUMBLE DRYER SHEETS

The cleaning world's best-kept secret, tumble dryer sheets are so versatile. As well as keeping your washing smelling good, they are great for so many household tasks. The beauty of them is that you can actually use them again after they have been used in the dryer. Here are a few simple and effective ideas:

IN THE BATHROOM ...

Soap scum scourer
Wipe away soap scum from your shower screen using a tumble dryer sheet.

Chrome shiner
Buff chrome with a tumble dryer sheet for a brilliant shine.

AROUND THE HOUSE ...

Car freshener
Tuck a few tumble dryer sheets under car seats to keep musty car odours at bay.

Suitcase freshener
After a trip abroad and before storing your suitcase, line the bottom with a few tumble dryer sheets. The next time you use it, it will smell lovely and fresh.

Drawer liner
Line drawers with a few tumble dryer sheets to keep your clothes smelling fresh. This is particularly useful for underwear drawers.

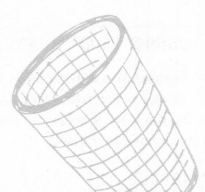

Cushion freshener

Zip a tumble dryer sheet into each of your sofa cushions to keep them smelling fresh.

Lifting dog hair

Rub your sofa with a tumble dryer sheet to pick up dog hairs.

Dusting blinds

Use a tumble dryer sheet instead of a duster to clean wooden slatted blinds. The sheet will lift the dirt rather than push it around.

Wastepaper basket liner

To keep your bin smelling fresh, line the bottom with a tumble dryer sheet.

Shoe freshener

Line smelly trainers or shoes with a tumble dryer sheet so the next time you wear them they smell fresh and clean.

Dusting electrical appliances

The electrical charge of televisions and computers mean they are terrible for attracting dust. If you dust them with a tumble dryer sheet, the dust won't re-settle for a few days.

USING TOOTHPASTE

Toothpaste is a daily essential for almost every single person on the planet. It whitens, brightens, and cleans your teeth and tongue, but did you know it has many other uses, particularly when it comes to cleaning your home?

AROUND THE HOUSE ...

Clean up white trainers

White trainers may seem like a good idea at the time, but a few trips outside often makes you think twice about your purchase. If your trainers have white rubber trims that have become discoloured over time, grab some white toothpaste and apply directly to the dirty area with a cloth.

Remove scuffs from shoes

A little toothpaste goes a long way when it comes to scuffed leather shoes. Just squeeze a small bit onto the scuffed area and rub with a soft cloth. Wipe clean with a damp cloth – easy peasy.

Clean a sticky iron

Is your iron sticky and no longer performing as well as it should? Gel toothpaste is the answer. It acts as the perfect mild abrasive for removing the gunk found on a well-used iron. Apply a layer to your iron, scrub off with a clean rag and rinse well.

Brighten car headlights

You won't realise how dirty and foggy your headlights are until you've tried this toothpaste hack! Rub some toothpaste onto the headlights with a damp paper towel and gently buff in a circular motion.

Remove crayon and felt pen marks from walls

Squirt the toothpaste directly onto the wall and start scrubbing. The fine abrasive in the toothpaste will rub away the crayon every time. Rinse with water and voilà!

USING FABRIC CONDITIONER

Fabric conditioner is one of those amazing products that reduces static cling as well as softening. It's perfect for many cleaning tasks. The added bonus is that fabric conditioner smells wonderful too!

IN THE KITCHEN ...

Hard water stains
Fabric conditioner is great at tackling hard water stains, which can be difficult to remove. Apply neat fabric conditioner to the stain, leave for 10 minutes and then rinse with warm water to achieve amazing results.

Baked-on grime
Stop the scrubbing and soak your baked-on casserole dishes with a squirt of fabric conditioner and warm water. Soak for at least 1 hour for a sparkly clean finish.

Scuff marks

A tiny drop of fabric conditioner mixed with water and very gently rubbed against painted walls and skirting boards will easily remove annoying marks.

Cleaning paint brushes

After doing a bit of DIY and freshening up your paintwork, apply some fabric conditioner direct to your brushes and let them soak for 10 minutes in a jar of water. The paint will come away in no time. This is the easiest way to get your brushes looking like new again.

Make your own tumble dryer sheets

Cut up a few square sponges and soak in a plastic tub of fabric conditioner. Keep the tub in your laundry room for ease and add a piece of sponge to your tumble dryer whenever you need to.

Wallpaper removal

Removing old wallpaper isn't always easy. Add a capful of fabric conditioner to a bowl of warm water to make removing old wallpaper a breeze. Sponge it over the required area and let it soak in for a good 20 minutes, then it will easily peel away.

USING DENTURE TABLETS

Bleaching agents are a common ingredient in denture tablets. This is what makes them a great cleaning tool, especially for toilets.

IN THE BATHROOM ...

Cleaning the toilet

This is a good tip for overnight cleaning. Simply drop a denture tablet into your toilet and leave overnight. This will remove any limescale and water mark stains.

Unblocking the drain

If your pipes are draining slower than they should be, add a couple of denture tablets and pour down some hot water.

AROUND THE HOUSE ...

Brightening diamonds

Add a denture tablet to a drop of warm water, then place your diamond jewellery in the solution. Allow to sit for a few minutes, then rinse.

USING COFFEE

Coffee is not just for drinking. You can keep used coffee grounds, as they are handy too.

IN THE KITCHEN ...

Fridge deodoriser
Got a bad smell in your fridge or freezer? Fill up some bowls with used coffee grounds and put them in the fridge or freezer overnight. It's an easy way to get rid of the stink.

Drain cleaning
Does your drain smell? Pour coffee granules down the drain and follow up with boiling water to help get rid of odours. Lovely stuff!

Hand cleaner
After chopping garlic or onions, your hands might be slightly stinky. Don't worry, those trusty coffee granules will come to your rescue. Just give your hands a rub with some granules or freshly ground coffee to help absorb the smelly odours.

AROUND THE HOUSE ...

Air freshener

Do you love, love, LOVE the smell of fresh coffee? Use it as an air freshener! All you need is a pretty fabric drawstring bag (or even an odd sock and an elastic band) and some delicious smelling coffee beans (or granules). Spoon the coffee beans into the bag, close it tightly and hang it up where it can't be seen, e.g. the back of door handles.

Keep insects at bay

If you've discovered insects coming into your home in the summer months, grab some ground coffee to keep them at bay, placing some bowls of it at entry points. When abroad, it's great to put a dish on your balcony to stop the mosquitoes coming in. Give it a try.

USING LINT ROLLERS

I love lint rollers – they are such a practical tool for helping to keep the house in order. Super-sticky, lightweight and cheap, they make quick work of picking up life's tiny messes. I highly recommend having a stock of them in your cleaning cupboard or, better still, stash a few away in the drawers of every room so they are always to hand.

A little bit of common sense before we get started: always use a new sheet for each task. As soon as the lint roller is dirty, and they do get dirty quickly, remove the sheet and continue with a fresh one.

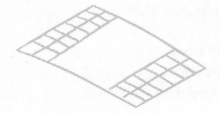

AROUND THE HOUSE ...

Picking up glitter
Removing glitter from surfaces is a real pain. Many vaccums struggle to pick up glitter, so it can be left for days, attach itself to people's feet and then make its way around your home. Grab a lint roller and zip up those sparkling particles – it's so easy.

Broken glass
It can be tough to clean away the small shards after picking up the bigger pieces of broken glass. Instead of putting your fingers at risk, run a lint roller over the area to pick up any small pieces.

Cleaning sound speakers and appliance dust grills
It's always hard work to clean speakers and the dust grills on appliances such as hairdryers – you can end up causing damage by pushing dust further into the mesh. A gentle run over with a lint roller can remove dust without causing any damage.

Dusting soft toys
Soft, fluffy toys can be covered in dust particles. Run a lint roller over them to keep them dust-free and help prevent musty smells.

Lampshades

I use a lint roller to remove dust from my lampshades. Vacuuming them will generally pull the shade out of shape and a damp cloth may create water marks. For dust-free lampshades, run a lint roller over them at least twice a week.

Bag interiors

All the crumbs and tiny pieces of lint that accumulate inside bags or purses can easily be removed with a lint roller.

Rugs

If you vacuum is struggling to pick up small bits, then roll the lint roller over.

Cars

There are lots of nooks and crannies in cars, between and below the seats, on the dashboard, and in the doors, where lots of little particles, crumbs and dust accumulates, especially if you have kids. A lint roller can really help clean these up.

Curtains

A lint roller can make the dusting of curtains so easy. Simply work on a section at a time.

Removing dandruff from clothing

If you are a dandruff sufferer, lint rollers are a great way to remove white flakes from your shoulders. They are easy enough to carry around in your bag or briefcase, too.

Christmas tree clean-up

Use a lint roller to pick up fallen needles from your Christmas tree.

Grooming a snooker table

Snooker tables can be really difficult to clean. Don't reach for a brush, grab a lint roller and go over it to get all the dust and any grime off. Rack up!

Clean out drawers

When cleaning drawers, after the contents have been removed, instead of whipping out the vacuum, give the empty drawers a quick zip over with a lint roller.

Bug disposal

If you are squeamish around dead bugs, such as the ones that you find around the window sills, use a lint roller to pick up their bodies and dispose of them easily.

And finally... your clothes!

Use your lint roller for its intended purpose – removing marks and fluff from your clothing.

SIMPLE TIPS FOR HOUSHOLD CLEANING

Practical methods for everyday jobs

In this section, I offer advice on how to do household chores in the most effective and efficient way.

Before you start, here are some general tips I advise for undertaking any cleaning job:

+ Wear comfortable clothing.
+ If you have long hair, it is always a good idea to tie it back.
+ Ensure you have all the tools and products you are going to need before you start.
+ Turn off distractions, such as your phone or the television.
+ Open the windows.
+ Whack on some of your favourite tunes or even an audio book, so you have something positive to listen to while you are in cleaning mode.
+ Always start with a declutter.
+ Begin cleaning at the top of the room and work downwards.

Keeping dust at bay

Do you find that when you dust your home, by the very next day the dust is back and you feel that all your hard work has gone to waste? Dusting the entire house is a big job. However, if you plan properly, you can get the job done in no time and the dust won't be back nearly as quickly. It is important to prepare your home for dusting and then work your way through the house from the top to the bottom.

Dust is detrimental to your family's health: asthma, eczema, COPD, threadworms, hayfever and allergies are all triggered by dust. It also attracts mites, bugs and roaches that bring a whole host of their own diseases. In addition, if you leave the dust, it turns into nasty, sticky, hard-to-remove grime!

TOOLS

Choose dusting tools that will grab the dust as opposed to ones that merely push it around. A feather duster may be fun to use or look fancy, but for serious dusting use a microfibre cloth. Microfibre cloths grab dust, are super-absorbent, streak-free and don't leave lint behind. Use your favourite multipurpose spray or furniture polish, whatever you feel is appropriate for the surfaces. If you do like to use a duster brush for a quick clean up, invest in a good-quality one that dust will stick to.

DECLUTTER

In order to make the dusting process easier and more effective, remove all the clutter from around the house. Make sure to remove things that have gathered on tables or worktops and never dust around clutter. If you're going to do the dusting, you may as well do it properly.

DUST IN THE RIGHT DIRECTION

When dusting a room, start at the highest point and work your way around the room down to the lowest point. Dust falls downwards like snow, so starting at the top prevents you from having to do the same areas again. Work clockwise, in a spiral or circular pattern. First, tackle all four corners of the ceiling, then move down to the light fittings, which will need a dry dust with a microfibre cloth. Next, move down to the door frames, picture rail and the tops of mirrors or picture frames. The furniture comes next, then finish by doing the skirting boards. Finally, grab the vacuum to collect the dust that has fallen on the floor.

CEILINGS, WALLS, DOOR FRAMES AND SKIRTING BOARDS

These areas can hold an amazing amount of dust, especially if you don't dust them on a regular basis. For best results, use a flat mop with a microfibre pad. For door frames and skirting boards, I use a mixture of warm water and a tiny amount of fabric conditioner. This removes scuff marks as well as the dust and leaves your home smelling fresh and clean.

CURTAINS AND BLINDS

These can hold a lot of dust if ignored. To keep the build-up to a minimum, be sure to vacuum both sides of your curtains on a weekly basis. Taking them down and shaking them thoroughly outside also helps to remove a lot of the dust. Try to have them dry cleaned at least once a year. Alternatively, when buying curtains try to opt for machine-washable ones.

For blinds, first close them completely. Starting at the top of each blind and working your way down, dust horizontally. I also find tumble dryer sheets (even ones that have already been used in the dryer) are fantastic for dusting blinds (see page 40).

UPHOLSTERED FURNITURE

After removing any pillows and cushions from sofas and chairs, vacuum them using the upholstery tool and the crevice tool for corners and edges. If cushion covers are removable, wash them monthly to freshen them up. If not, take a microfibre cloth dampened with water and a very small amount of washing-up liquid, then gently wipe, working in stripes up and down the area, to prevent water marks. Finally, spray with a fabric refresher (shop-bought or see page 19).

ELECTRONICS

Computers, televisions, DVD players, music players and printers are notorious dust magnets. Always unplug the equipment before cleaning. A gentle swipe with a slightly damp microfibre cloth usually does the job, but if your vacuum has brush attachments, a gentle vacuum certainly won't hurt. Be sure to vacuum the dust from around the cords and vents to keep devices from getting clogged and overheating.

LAMPSHADES

Rub a lint roller over lampshades – it's a quick fix and will effortlessly pick up the dust without damaging the shade.

DELICATE ITEMS OR AREAS THAT YOU CAN'T SEE WELL

Delicate items or hard-to-see areas can be vacuumed with a pair of old tights placed over the vacuum nozzle. This will collect the dust but eliminates the risk of sucking up valuables or other items you don't want vacuumed up or damaging delicate things such as ceiling light fittings.

For all your stylish ornaments and other intricate items where dust can get trapped, lightly mist with clean water and gently brush with a clean natural-bristled paintbrush or a make-up brush.

Vents
Use your vacuum with the brush attachment to suck up the dust in air vents. If the space is really small, another good trick is to use an old mascara brush!

Keyboards
Use the sticky edge of a Post-it note to pick up gunk between the keys on keyboards. You will be amazed at what comes out!

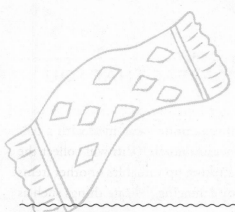

DOOR MATS

Shaking out your door mats and quickly sweeping under them takes less than a minute and will save lots more time on dusting and vacuuming.

STAIR EDGES

The edges of wooden stair treads is another place where dust frequently and quickly collects. Most of us don't vacuum the stairs more than once a week, but by dusting the stair edges with a microfibre duster, it will stop dust spreading around the house. As you go up the stairs, take a cloth with you and quickly go over the edges of the treads – this will really help keep the dust at bay.

Kitchen cleaning

Cluttered cabinets, a dusty fridge top, and an oven that smokes every time you use it are not the components of an ideal kitchen. Your kitchen takes a lot of wear and tear, so it's important to give it a more intense clean every so often.

BEFORE YOU START, ORGANISE AND PREPARE

+ Remove all the items on worktops and other visible surfaces and put them to one side in another room or on your kitchen table for the time being. This includes moveable electrical items such as smoothie makers and toasters.
+ Ensure that you start with clean and dry dishes, pans, crockery and cutlery. If anything is dirty, wash it up first and remove to a separate room so it is not in the way.
+ Remove used tea towels and put them in the wash.
+ Remove and empty the bin.
+ Open the window – it's always good to have fresh air when you are cleaning.
+ Shake any door mats and leave outside or pop in the washing machine on a low temperature wash.

GET CLEANING

+ As always, I advise to start cleaning at the top of the room and then work your way down. Dust down the ceiling with a flat-headed long-handled dry mop or duster. Ensure you also dust the corners of walls and the light fittings.

+ Determine whether the walls need to be washed, especially in dirty spots such as behind the kitchen bin.

+ Empty the kitchen cupboards one at a time. Wash them out with warm soapy water. For any sticky patches, lightly spray with neat white wine vinegar (or use your 50:50 spray bottle solution of water and vinegar) and leave for 10 minutes to work, then rinse. Don't forget to pay attention to the door, both inside and out, and clean the handle. If you have high gloss kitchen cabinets, after cleaning buff them with a cloth and spray of glass cleaner to really bring out the shine.

+ Run the dishwasher on empty. Add a little vinegar or bicarbonate of soda to the empty dishwasher unit and a squeeze of neat lemon juice into the detergent compartment before running it. If your dishwasher has a food trap in the bottom, clean it out. Wash down the outside of the dishwasher.

+ Wash down all the worktops, tiles and splashbacks.

+ Give the hob a clean. If it is stainless steel, buff with baby oil to get the perfect shine. If the loose components, such as the pan supports and the burner caps, are greasy, pop them into a small sandwich bag with the tiniest squirt of oven cleaner, seal and leave for 10 minutes. After this time, give them a rinse to bring them up like new.

+ Get down on your hands and knees and tackle those cupboard baseboards with a bowl of warm soapy water. These take a lot of wear and tear from the vacuum and your feet.

- ✦ Wash down the sink area and don't forget to clean the drain using my solution of bicarbonate of soda and white wine vinegar (see page 20). Remember to flush it with water to keep those drains fresh and odour free.

- ✦ Give the oven a really good clean. Remove the shelves and place in the bath. If the oven interior is very dirty, use an oven scraper to remove as much of the greasy build-up as possible, dampen the interior, then apply a good layer of bicarbonate of soda and spray with white wine vinegar. Close the oven door and allow these two amazing staples to work together for at least 1 hour. Soak the shelves in the same solution in your bath. Afterwards, rinse everything clean with warm water.

- ✦ Your microwave will also need a little attention. In order to save it getting too messy in the first place, try to remember to wipe it down after each use. However, for a deep clean, the best method is to place a slice of lemon into a bowl of water. Place this in the microwave and set on full power for 5 minutes. After this time, wipe it down. The grease will just lift away and your microwave will smell so good.

- Empty the fridge. Sort through the food and check all the 'best before' and 'use by' dates. If you have any old jars of food stored at the back, toss them! Warm soapy water is the best solution for cleaning the fridge. Soak the shelves in warm soapy water over the sink and give the fridge interior a really good clean. Use an ear bud to get into the rubber seal and remove any bits of old food.
- Wipe over the sides and lid of the kitchen bin. Use a small toothbrush to get into the smaller areas on the lid, if needed.
- The final job is to give the floor a really good clean. I use a floor cleaner or steamer rather than a mop (which tends to push the dirt around). I also use diluted floor cleaner – too much neat product causes smears and stickiness, so make sure you always dilute well.

Now you can move everything back to its proper place. There is something quite satisfying about a clean kitchen. When perfect order is restored, order a takeaway and enjoy the clean space for a few hours before the chaos of modern family life takes over again.

How to de-scale
the kettle

We all use the kettle on a near-daily basis, for anything from boiling water for cooking to filling hot water bottles, and – of course – making hot beverages such as tea and coffee. The British are a famous nation of tea-drinkers – we go through 120 million cups of tea every single day. Imagine the amount of grime accumulating in all those kettles! Limescale builds up in kettles really quickly. Limescale (or calcium carbonate) is a tough, milky white deposit, which is primarily found in places where hot water has evaporated. The deposits are unsightly and are difficult to remove by scrubbing alone, making cleaning the kettle a bit of a challenge.

Regular de-scaling will prolong the life of your kettle and I recommend that you do it on a monthly basis. There are many products on the market that work really well, but I prefer to de-scale my kettle using more natural ingredients, such as vinegar or lemon juice. After all, the water from the kettle is what we drink. If I'm using lemon juice, I tend to use the bottles of ready-squeezed lemon juice from the supermarket cooking aisle, rather than using real lemons – it's more cost effective.

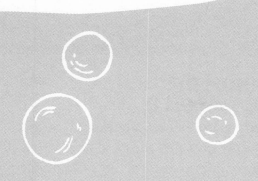

De-scaling is an easy process – just follow these very simple steps:

1. Fill the kettle with half white wine vinegar or lemon juice and half cold water.

2. Leave for 1 hour.

3. Bring the kettle (with the solution still inside) to the boil.

4. Empty the kettle. The limescale will come away with the water.

5. Re-fill the kettle with cold water.

6. Boil again.

7. Empty the kettle once more, then it's ready to use as normal.

TIP

Whenever you are cleaning down your work surfaces, always wipe over the outside of your kettle too, to keep it looking clean and shiny.

Bathroom cleaning

Which room in the house do you like cleaning the least? I'll bet you said the bathroom, didn't you? Faced with a soapy shower screen, a bath with a rim of soap scum and the dreaded toilet, bathrooms are one of the worst places in the home for germs and bacteria to really spread. A good bathroom clean takes both time and elbow grease, but you can clean your bathrooms quickly and efficiently by using my easy process.

Before you start, organise and prepare

+ Remove the laundry basket, if that is where you keep it.
+ Remove all bath towels and bathroom mats and pop them in the wash.
+ Remove the shower curtain, if you have one, and put it in the washing machine on a low temperature with some white wine vinegar. This will tackle any traces of mould.
+ Clear the surfaces of all products, plants or candles and put them outside the room so they are not in the way.
+ Empty all cabinets of toiletries.
+ Don't forget to open the window. When cleaning the bathroom you are going to be using some toxic products, so it is very important to stay safe.

GET CLEANING

+ Work downwards from the top of the room. Start by dusting the ceiling with a flat-headed long-handled dry mop or duster to remove all the cobwebs. Pay extra attention to the corners.
+ Dust the light fitting using a long duster.
+ Remove the vent and extractor fan covers, if you have them, and soak them in warm water with a drop of washing-up liquid. While they are soaking, clean the fan and vent well with a small toothbrush or mascara brush. Then dry the covers and pop them back on.
+ Clean the window and any mirrors with glass or window cleaner. If your mirrors have bad water marks, rub over these with a halved lemon. Leave the lemon juice on for about 15 minutes, then rinse with a clean wet cloth. Use a separate dry cloth to buff dry.
+ Clean inside all the cupboards and cabinets with a multi-purpose bathroom spray or my homemade all-purpose cleaning solution (see page 17). Don't forget to clean the doors and the door handles. Also reach up high to clean the tops of the cabinets, as thick dust can settle there.
+ Clean the toilet (see pages 72-73 for detailed instructions). Pay attention to the base of the toilet and the surrounding pipes, as well as the bowl. Give the seat a really good wipe over and don't forget to use the right cloth (BLUE FOR LOO). After cleaning, add some toilet bleach.
+ If you have any limescale on the taps, cut a lemon in half and firmly push the lemon over the nozzle of the tap so that it stays on. Leave it for a few hours before rinsing. Copper cloths are also great for tackling limescale on taps.
+ Vacuum or sweep the floor.

- Use a mixture of warm water and detergent to scrub the floor tiles. Rinse with clear warm water, then use a dry cloth to polish dry.
- Use the same type of mixture to scrub the wall tiles, then wipe down with a squeegee and use a dry cloth to polish dry.
- If you have discoloured tile grout, mix together a thick paste of bicarbonate of soda and white wine vinegar. Apply the paste to the grout with a small brush or an old toothbrush, leave for 15 minutes to settle and then rinse. Your grout will come up as good as new.
- For the plug holes, use a drain cleaner or apply a heaped spoonful of bicarbonate of soda to each plug hole and pour down some white wine vinegar. Leave for 15 minutes, then flush with water.
- Clean the shower door/screen, sides/tiles and base thoroughly. For any mould build-up, treat with neat white wine vinegar. Once you've finished, give everything a good wipe down with your squeegee.
- To clean limescale from the shower head, use a small plastic bag filled with white wine vinegar tied over the head (see page 74).
- Don't forget to clean the shower hose/flex and the fixtures and control switches/taps.
- Clean the bathroom light switch or cord. To whiten the cord, mix together a paste of bicarbonate of soda and white wine vinegar and rub this over the cord with your fingers. Leave for 15 minutes, then rinse off.
- Clean the bath with a multipurpose spray or with a homemade solution of 50:50 white wine vinegar and water. Again, tackle any mould with neat white wine vinegar, leaving it on for a little a while to do its work before rinsing.

FINISHING UP

+ Put all the toiletries and items back in cupboards and on the sides.
+ Bring the colour back into your bathroom by bringing in clean towels, mats, accessories and plants.
+ If you are at home, light a few scented candles to mask the smell of the cleaning products.
+ Leave the window ajar to keep the air circulating.

Tip

I always keep a little caddy of cleaning products in the bathroom, so that I can give it a quick whizz-over after using without having to go up and down the stairs to get products. Squeegees are your bathroom's best friend. Keep a squeegee in the shower so that you can wipe away the water after showering – this will prevent the build-up of water marks and limescale.

HOW TO CLEAN THE TOILET

Keeping the toilet clean is a must for any busy household – stopping the spread of nasty germs and reducing health risks. A dirty toilet can contaminate the rest of the bathroom, leaving bacteria and germs to spread around freely. A daily wipe down isn't always enough. Make a point to give your toilets a really good deep clean weekly and always put the toilet seat down when flushing (otherwise germs can escape into your bathroom, latching on to towels and toothbrushes).

Here's how to clean your toilets properly:

1 Lift the toilet seat and start with cleaning the bowl. Squirt bleach or toilet cleaner right under the rim and let it run down the bowl. Then, with your toilet brush or a plastic flexible D-shaped brush to get right under the rim and into those awkward U-bends, scrub away, covering the whole bowl in the product. Leave to soak for a few minutes.
2 Meanwhile, focus on the seat and the outside of the toilet. Use a good disinfectant bathroom spray and a clean cloth and start wiping from the top of your toilet, working your way down. Then, with a fresh cloth and warm water, rinse and buff the seat and the outside of the toilet.
3 Time to go back to the bowl. Give it one last scrub before you flush.
4 Add in some more toilet cleaner or bleach and leave.
5 Finally, add a toilet capsule to your cistern. These are great for keeping limescale at bay – I tend to add a new one in weekly.

NOTE: if you find you have any brown staining at the bottom of the bowl, my trick is to remove as much water from the bowl as possible. It's not the most pleasant experience, but toilet bowl marks can be unsightly – you really don't want any visitors seeing them. Either use a plunger to push the water through the pipe or use an old cup to empty it out yourself. Add a neat limescale remover, put the toilet seat down and leave it to work overnight. Be sure not to mix the limescale remover with any other product as this can be very dangerous. If you would prefer to try a more natural approach, you could use cola (see Tip, below).

I do clean my toilets a lot, but I find that if you keep on top of your cleaning, it becomes much easier. Little and often is the key.

Tip

If you want to use a less toxic product, try using cola soft drink. Cola is an amazing cleaner and will help get rid of rust and limescale quickly and effectively. And YES, this really does work! Try it.

Simply pour 1 glass of cola into the toilet and leave for 1 hour before flushing. If you have limescale and rust stains in the toilet bowl, soak an old cloth in cola, then rub this all over the toilet bowl by hand. Alternatively, use your toilet brush to spread it around. Again, leave for 1 hour or overnight. The acid in the cola will break down the stains. Then either scrub again, if the limescale was bad, or just flush away.

HOW TO CLEAN
A SHOWER HEAD WITH VINEGAR

When your shower head starts looking crusty, you have more to worry about than just the nasty appearance – your showers may also become less luxurious if the water can't get through holes plugged up with limescale. There is a tried and true method for removing limescale from shower heads, and the best part is that you don't even have to remove the fixture! Just grab a bottle of white wine vinegar, a small plastic sandwich bag, and a piece of string.

1 Fill the plastic bag part-way with white wine vinegar.
2 Place the bag over the shower head until the entire fixture is fully immersed in the vinegar.
3 Fasten the bag with a piece of string, wrapping it securely around the neck of the shower head.
4 Leave it to soak for several hours, or overnight for an especially dirty fixture. NOTE: if you have a brass-, gold-, or nickel-coated shower head, remove it from the vinegar after 30 minutes – any longer and it could damage the finish.
5 Untie the bag and remove it from the shower head.
6 Scrub the fixture with an old toothbrush if any deposits remain. Focus on the areas around the holes where the water comes out.
7 Turn the hot water back on to flush out even more residue. Repeat this process until you no longer see mineral deposits.
8 Polish and dry the shower head with a soft cloth, to remove any water spots and help the shower head look like new.

Bed care

Your bedroom should be a clean, calm and organised place to rest your head at the end of a long day. Having a comfortable, well-made bed to climb into will make all the difference to the way you feel.

To keep a bed in the best possible condition, I recommend the following:

+ a breathable cotton mattress pad/protector
+ 2 pillow protector covers
+ a breathable duvet
+ firm pillows
+ good-quality bedding

Although you can wash both mattresses and pillows, it can be a big job and they can take a while to dry, so the less often you have to do this, the better. A mattress protector will guard your mattress against the effects of dust, spills and sweat stains, but also provides an extra layer of comfort. Pillow protectors will act in the same way, prolonging the life of your pillows.

HANDY HINT

I don't think there is such thing as too many pillows! However, when styling pillows on the bed, think in odd numbers: three, five or seven pillows will remove symmetry and add interest to the eye.

Change and wash the bedding (including the protectors) once a week.

+ Vacuum the mattress each time you change your sheets.
+ Freshen the mattress with a light dusting of bicarbonate of soda mixed with lavender essential oil to soak up any sweaty odours, followed by a good vacuum, every 2 weeks. Lavender is a great essential oil to use in the bedroom as it helps aid sleep and will help relax you.
+ Clean the mattress with a carpet cleaning product and upholstery tool every 6 months.
+ Wash pillows every 6 months or discard and purchase new ones.
+ Store winter/summer duvets in vacuum packs, adding in a few tumble dryer sheets to keep them smelling fresh.

HOW TO MAKE THE BED

Fitted sheet

Most of us choose fitted sheets for ease these days. Slip the corners of the sheet over your mattress. I always pick the mattress up at the corner, then rest it on my knee so that I can really pull the fitted sheet into position – there is nothing worse than a badly fitted sheet moving around in the night. Make sure the sheet is pulled tight over the mattress and smooth out any gaps or bunches.

Flat sheet

Next comes the (optional) flat sheet. Lay the flat sheet on top of the fitted sheet, with the finished side facing down. To get that super-crisp and tucked-in look, make hospital corners (see below), then fold over the top of the flat sheet and tuck in.

To make hospital corners, first tuck the flat sheet in at the foot of the bed, ensuring it sits smoothly. At one corner, pick the edge of the sheet up and, pulling it tautly, place it on the surface of the bed, forming a triangle shape. Tuck the loose corner hanging down under the mattress. Holding the sheet in place against the side of the mattress with your free hand, fold the sheet resting on the bed over and down and tuck it in neatly, then tuck in the sheet all along the side of the bed. Repeat on the other side.

Pillows

Fluff the feathers or pillow filling by 'chopping' the pillow down the middle with your arm, then fold it in half lengthways to make it easier to insert into the pillowcase. From the outside of the pillowcase, pinch a corner of the pillow and pull the case down.

Sofa care

Depending on how we use the sofa, it can take a lot of wear and tear, from eating TV dinners to watching a film with your pet snuggled up against you. The couch can capture body oils, cooking odours, dust mites and other allergens and they will all be lurking there causing allergies and general irritation to airways. Eating on your sofa really isn't ideal – food particles, sticky finger marks and spilt drinks can all occur from enjoying a snack on the sofa. Keep eating at the table. If you do like to indulge on your sofa, you need to keep it clean or at least cover with a washable throw.

Vacuum the sofa weekly and invest in a good upholstery cleaner or leather cleaner. When vacuuming, take all of the cushions off and get to every part of the sofa. Remove cushion covers, if you can, and wash them as often as possible.

Always puff up your sofa cushions before bedtime – sofas can easily lose their shape and an untidy-looking sofa can really ruin the effect of your whole room.

MY TOP SOFA CLEANING TIPS

Bicarbonate of soda is great for a lot of things, including the removal of grime and embedded dirt from your sofa. It is safe for most types of upholstery, but test the fabric first in an inconspicuous area. You will need a stiff brush, bicarbonate of soda, antibacterial spray or fabric refresher, and your vacuum cleaner with the smaller brush attachment. A steamer is optional.

+ Use the stiff brush to brush away crumbs, dust and other debris.
+ Sprinkle the sofa with bicarbonate of soda (you could also mix it with an essential oil if you like) and leave it for 20–30 minutes.
+ Use the brush attachment on your vacuum to thoroughly remove the bicarbonate of soda.
+ If you have a steamer, give your sofa a very light steam to kill germs. Always hold it about 30 cm/12 inches away from the fabric.
+ Finish off with an antibacterial spray or a fabric refresher.
+ To speed up the drying process, open the windows. Alternatively, on a cold winter day, a hair dryer can help.
+ For any tough stains that are still present, mix together 180 ml/¾ cup warm water with 60 ml/¼ cup white wine vinegar and 1 tablespoon washing-up liquid. Scrub the mixture in with a hard brush and then blot dry with kitchen paper or a clean cloth.

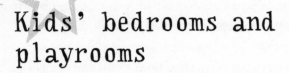

Kids' bedrooms and playrooms

One of the biggest arguments in many households is the state of the kids' bedrooms and playrooms. We often battle with our children on how to get these rooms spick and span, while they whine and moan – it's exhausting for everyone. However, there are better ways than shouting or scolding to get your kids to clean their own rooms.

SET A GOOD EXAMPLE

Don't live by the phrase 'do as I say, not as I do'. Kids are too percep-tive to accept that they must clean their room while their parents' room remains unkempt. If you take pride in your home and keep your own things in order, it's the first step towards encouraging your kids to do the same. I believe my own organised ways come from growing up in a clean and tidy house.

BE ORGANISED AND MAKE A PLACE FOR EVERYTHING

Purchase storage tubs and toy boxes with lids, so items can easily be put away. If your child has a raised bed, pick storage boxes that can easily slide neatly under the bed. Also, consider storage boxes that double as seating. Use a hanging pocket organiser to house both art supplies and small items that would get lost in bigger bins. When implementing a storage system, involve the children so that they know where to put their favourite toys. Consider adjusting the height of the wardrobe rods, low enough so that your kids can hang up their own clothes. Use picture-hanging wire and clothes pegs to display their art handiwork.

KEEP IT OFF THE FLOOR

Playrooms and bedrooms are spaces for playing, learning and creating — none of which can be accomplished if there's only a little bit of floor space available. Instead of reducing space by covering the floor with bins and bookshelves, try wall-mounted storage.

CREATE A DESIGNATED SPACE FOR CERTAIN ACTIVITIES

Try to create a specific designated space for each activity that together makes a cohesive play area. Paint a wall with chalkboard paint for an art corner. Keep a stack of comfy pillows or beanbags next to a wall-mounted bookshelf for a fun reading nook. By designating areas for each activity, it also makes it easier to clean up. When you say to your child 'let's clean up the art corner', you won't get a blank stare as they try to figure out whether the sticker-covered couch or the box of lidless markers under the stairs is the 'art corner'.

DON'T EXPECT PERFECTION

It's not going to happen. The caps aren't going back on the right colour marker every time. There will be days when, despite your best efforts, it looks like an artistic, tower-building hurricane ripped through the playroom. You have too much going on in your life to stress out about one room in your house. You *can* just close the door. Don't panic – choose what works for you and your family and start small. You'll be amazed what you can accomplish.

Easy-to-miss areas

Just because you can't see the dirt, that doesn't mean it isn't there. In fact, it's those hidden areas in each room of your home that are often the dirtiest of all. I have listed here a few areas that even I miss when doing my cleaning:

+ **Inside drawers** Empty each drawer in your kitchen and bathroom one at a time and vacuum out what remains. If necessary, use a damp cloth to clean up any spills and allow to dry before replacing the contents. Keep drawers smelling fresh by adding a little bag of lavender.
+ **Cooker-hood fan** Place your filters in a clean sink filled with very hot or boiling water and add a large spoonful of bicarbonate of soda. Soak for 30 minutes, then carefully remove and rinse with clean water. Allow the filters to dry before replacing.
+ **Sliding door and window tracks** Remove loose debris by vacuuming and use an old, dry toothbrush to dislodge the rest. If necessary, sprinkle with a light dusting of bicarbonate of soda and spray with a mixture of white wine vinegar and water. Leave for 5 minutes, then wipe away the grime with a clean microfibre cloth.
+ **Air filters and vents** Replace your air filter every 6–8 weeks, as needed. Remove vent covers and vacuum dust and debris from inside the vents before replacing the covers.
+ **Indoor plants** Cleaning methods will depend on the type of plant – this can range from a gentle wipe of the leaves with a soft, damp cloth, to giving plants a light spray with a shower head or garden hose.
+ **Underneath furniture** Dust and dirt love to hide under beds, sofas, and other large pieces of furniture. A long-handled dust mop works well on hard surfaces. For carpeted areas, you may need to use your vacuum cleaner or move the furniture to access the dirt.

Beginner's guide to laundry

When we first move out of home and are suddenly faced with doing the laundry alone, it can be a really daunting task. But laundry is something we just cannot avoid – we need to wear clean clothes, use clean towels and sleep in a nice clean bed. Here is some simple laundry advice:

SEPARATE YOUR LAUNDRY

Start by separating your laundry into different piles. A good way of helping you do this is to get a laundry basket that has sections. Take care not to put any clothes that are labelled 'dry clean only' into the washing piles.

Make 4 piles:

+ Bedding and towels
+ Jeans and other denim items
+ Shirts and thinner items of clothing (such as underwear)
+ Knitwear

These piles can be further separated by colour:

+ Whites
+ Light colours
+ Dark colours

You can also separate by fabric:

+ Cottons
+ Synthetics
+ Wool
+ Delicates

By separating into fabrics as well as colours you can choose the best cycle to use on your washing machine for each pile.

CHECK POCKETS

Always check the pockets of any clothing before you do any washing. There is nothing worse than washing cash or a tissue that was in someone's pocket.

TURN CLOTHING INSIDE OUT

To keep your clothes in better condition, always wash them inside out, to stop the colours fading. It is particularly important to wash jeans and dark colours inside out.

USE THE RIGHT WASHING DETERGENT

Make sure you choose your detergent wisely – don't be swayed by pretty bottles. There is a huge choice these days in the supermarkets, but you need to find one that is right for you and your machine. I find liquid detergent better than powder, as it's kinder to your washing machine and can also be used as a pre-stain treatment.

TREAT STAINS

Always treat stains before adding items to the wash. Use a pre-stain treatment and let it soak in for 15 minutes before putting items into the washing machine.

TEMPERATURE

Washing at lower temperatures is better for your clothes and will help prolong their life. It is also better for the environment. Try to wash everyday clothing no higher than 40°C.

TOWELS

The best way to wash towels is on a high heat – choose a 60°C setting.

+ Wash them separately from the rest of the laundry.
+ Do not use fabric conditioner as this will damage the fibres. Instead, add some white wine vinegar to the wash.
+ Always start the drying process for your towels as soon as the washing cycle has finished.

Laundry symbols

Always read the labels on clothing before washing. Here's a quick guide to the laundry symbols.

Normal wash	Gentle cycle wash
Wash in cold water	Wash in hot water
Hand wash only	Safe to bleach
Don't bleach	Tumble dry
Don't tumble dry	Dry clean
Don't dry clean	Don't iron
Don't steam	Hot iron

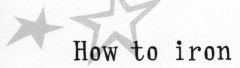

How to iron

Ironing – it's a bit like Marmite: you either love it or hate it! Personally, I love it. I find ironing is quite a good de-stresser and love nothing more than to put on a good film and spend an hour getting really stuck in. I know that I am achieving something worthwhile.

As much as some of us hate it, ironing is one of those jobs you should do most weeks, otherwise you will find the ironing pile starts to really get out of control.

You can make ironing easier and faster by following a few simple steps.

DOES IT NEED IRONING?

When you bring your washing in from the line or tumble dryer, remember that not every single item will need an iron. If you hang your washing well on the washing line and don't overload the tumble dryer, this can potentially save a garment from needing to be ironed. Rather than folding items into the ironing basket, some of them can be popped straight onto a hanger and put away in the wardrobe. I find that woollen jumpers don't need much of an iron and try to get these hung up straightaway.

SPLIT THE IRONING UP

Split your ironing into piles before you start. Take a look at the care labels and see what temperatures the garments need. If you are using an older iron, start by ironing the low-temperature items, such as silk, first and move up to the awkward creased items that need a higher heat last.

LIGHTS ON

Always iron in a well-lit room.

HANGERS AT THE READY

Have plenty of clothes hangers to hand and a little rail or some of those over-the-door ironing hooks, so that you can hang ironed garments up right away. For those items you won't be hanging, immediately fold them on a flat surface and put to one side, ready to go into drawers. This makes light work when it is time to put things away.

IRONING BOARD

Use a good sturdy ironing board that doesn't rock or wobble. Also make sure your board is at the right height for you.

Make sure you utilise the whole board by placing long items across the full width of the board. The thinner end of the ironing board can also be very useful: it's particularly good for getting to the creases near armholes. Place tops over the end of the board, being careful not to stretch the fabric.

IRON INSIDE OUT

Have you ever noticed a slight sheen on dark clothes post-ironing? This is caused by the heat of the iron. A simple way to avoid this is by ironing clothes inside out wherever possible. This will help protect the appearance of your garments and keep them looking great. Other fabrics you should iron inside out are: silk, satin, linen, denim and corduroy.

DON'T OVER-IRON

If your garment looks good after being ironed on just one side, don't bother ironing the other side. Not only will this save you time, but ironing may cause your clothes to look tired over time. Don't do more than you have to.

Avoid wiggling the iron around too much, as this may cause fabric to stretch. It may also create new creases in the fabric, which will be tough to remove.

STUBBORN CREASES

Stubborn creases may need a bit more than a hot iron. Make up a DIY spray from equal parts white wine vinegar and water. Spray directly onto badly creased areas and they should iron out more easily.

LOOK OUT FOR STAINS

If you spot a stain while ironing, do not iron over it – the heat from the iron will embed the stain even further. Instead, soak the garment in a bowl of cold water with a drop of white wine vinegar and then wash again.

PURE COTTON ITEMS

Pure (100 per cent) cotton garments are probably the hardest items to iron. Make your life easier by ironing these while they are still slightly damp. The heat will create steam when it hits the water, helping the creases to fall out.

IRON CARE

Make sure your iron has completely cooled down before you put it away. Also, empty out the water reservoir, so that limescale doesn't build up.

How to declutter

For many of us, the most overwhelming part of cleaning our homes is getting rid of the clutter. There are no two ways about it, decluttering your home can be a huge job. For so many people it seems that 'letting go' of their surplus belongings is the biggest hurdle to overcome – it stops them from properly finishing or even starting the decluttering process in the first place.

Our lives should not be so burdened with clutter. A minimalistic approach to life can be very uplifting both to the spirit and one's health. Besides, effective cleaning can be almost impossible if you home is full of clutter. You spend the time you have set aside to clean merely picking stuff up and tidying away old newspapers, magazines and toys. If your home is starting to feel cluttered and you find that you are struggling to locate your belongings when you need them, then you know that this is a job that you need to do.

My advice is to break your home into sections and tackle one section at a time:

+ Bedrooms
+ Bathrooms
+ Kitchen
+ Living rooms
+ Garage/garden shed

Plan some time to achieve these tasks – slot them into your diary. If you need help, ask for it. Involve other family members or ask a friend to help out. A weekend can be a practical time for tackling jobs such as the garage or the garden shed and you may want to choose a dry day to do these.

When it comes to decluttering, it's easy to take a negative approach. The worst way to tackle decluttering is to grab a box or a few bin bags and literally just throw stuff away in order to speed up the process. Decluttering needs a more positive approach. Evaluate each item before you make the decision to throw it away. Ask yourself:

+ Do I use it?
+ Do I need it?
+ Do I really want it?

If your answer is no to any of these questions, you should think about getting rid.

It helps to sort your items into piles:

+ Keep pile
+ Donate pile
+ Rubbish pile

Take the useable items to your local charity shop, have a car boot sale or use local social media selling sites to move them on. If your items are in good condition, it will give someone else a good turn to use them.

THE 5-MINUTE CHALLENGE

Baby steps are important for some people when decluttering. If the thought of dedicating a day or weekend to it is too much, then why not try my 5-minute declutter challenge? Even if it only makes a dent in your mountain, it's a start. Celebrate after you've made that start and be proud. Then, take another 5 minutes tomorrow... And another 5 minutes the day after that... Before you know it, you'll have cleared out a whole wardrobe or a room, then half your house. Before long, your house could be even more uncluttered than mine.

For those who are overwhelmed by their clutter, here are some great ways to get started, 5 minutes at a time:

+ **Paperwork** Choose a designated spot for incoming paperwork – a good place is a worktop in the kitchen or in the main family area. Invest in some storage that looks aesthetically pleasing – I like a wire basket and use it to keep school letters, mail, bills and those other bits and pieces that come in throughout the week. Then, dedicate 5 minutes a week to sorting through it.
+ **Pick a shelf** Take 5 minutes to evaluate what you have on it. Tidy it up and remove whatever is not needed or anything that has not been used in the last 6 months.

+ **Pick up 5 things** These should be things that you actually use, but that you just seem to put anywhere, because they don't have a home. Take a minute to think it through – where would be a good home? Then assign them a spot and stick to it.
+ **Clothes** When you are getting ready in the morning and looking through your wardrobe for something to wear, spend 5 minutes pulling out items that you haven't worn in a long time. If they are seasonal clothes, store them in vacuum storage bags or in under-bed storage bags. Get rid of the rest. Do this a little at a time, until your wardrobe only contains what you like to wear.

Pull everything out of a drawer. Just take the drawer out and empty it onto a table. Sort the items into 3 piles:

+ Stuff that really belongs in the drawer.
+ Stuff that belongs elsewhere.
+ Stuff to get rid of.

Clean the drawer, then replace the items from the first pile in a neat and orderly fashion. Deal with the other piles immediately!

Learn to love the uncluttered look. Once you've decluttered an area, take the time to enjoy it. It's a lovely look. Make that your standard! Learn to hate clutter! Then catch clutter and toss it, wherever it crops up.

50 things you need to chuck away

Don't be overwhelmed by the build-up of clutter in your home – be ruthless. I mean, do you really drink out of every single mug in your cupboard or do you just use a few? Turn it into a bit of a game and set yourself a goal. Here I have listed 50 things to chuck away. Check each category and go for it!

✦ Out-of-date newspaper and magazines
✦ Scraps of wrapping paper
✦ Old paperwork (make sure you shred anything with personal details on it)
✦ Takeaway menus that you don't use
✦ Birthday and Christmas cards
✦ Burnt-out candles
✦ Diffusers that have lost their scent
✦ Plastic food tubs that are discoloured
✦ Out-of-date tinned food
✦ Odd cutlery
✦ Mugs and glasses that don't match sets
✦ Tablemats that are peeling and look worn
✦ Recipe cards you don't use
✦ Old tea towels with holes
✦ Empty jars
✦ Empty boxes

- Medication that has expired
- Bathroom products that have expired or that you just don't use (see also pages 106-107)
- Odd socks
- Odd earrings
- Broken or scratched sunglasses
- Underwear that has frayed or has holes
- Worn-out hair bobbles
- Make-up that you don't wear
- Tatty make-up brushes
- Bedding that no longer matches your colour scheme
- Worn-out bath towels and mats
- Hair brushes with bristles missing
- Clothes that don't fit anymore
- Belts that are worn and close to breaking
- Battered handbags and purses
- Books you have read and won't read again
- DVDs that you won't watch again
- Dried flowers that look tatty
- Chipped ornaments
- Old mobile phones
- Old phone chargers
- Broken light bulbs
- Games consoles that no longer work or aren't played with
- Used batteries
- Broken toys
- Felt tips and pens that don't work
- Receipts
- Business cards
- Old family planners and calendars
- Post-it note messages
- Old format computer discs
- Used note pads
- Used ink cartridges
- Used gift cards

Chucking yourself in at the deep end like this will make you feel so much better. You will find it much easier to organise your home when you only have items you actually want and need. Don't forget to donate, recycle and sell, too.

Deodorising: how to keep your home smelling amazing!

We all love a clean, fresh-smelling home, but we sometimes don't get it. Smells from cooking, pets and the general wear and tear of daily life can get in the way and leave our homes smelling mustier than we would like. I love to have my windows open, so that bad odours can escape and fresh air can blow throughout my home. However, when the weather is temperamental, this simple trick isn't always possible.

Of course, the best way to combat odours is to get at them before they have had a chance to spread. Dirty dishes, an overlooked spillage, and old food in the fridge just exacerbate the odour issue. Keeping on top of removing odour-causing material will help keep your home smelling fresh and clean because it is fresh and clean!

I'm also a firm believer in maintaining a strict no shoes in the house policy. Shoes track in dirt, dirt gets ground into the floor, and that dirt smells.

Ensure you regularly vacuum your carpets and upholstery, take out the rubbish before it gets too smelly and follow a regular cleaning routine.

Here are a few more ideas to keep your home smelling fresh year-round:

ADD SCENT BOOSTERS
TO YOUR VACUUM

This is one of my favourite tips. If you follow my social media, you will have seen me do this plenty of times! Vacuum up a few laundry scent boosters and allow them to sit in the collection drum of your vacuum. As you vacuum, the scent will be released. Remember to change them weekly, each time you empty out your collection drum, and only use a few.

MAKE YOUR OWN
CHEMICAL-FREE AIR FRESHENER

This is very simple: fill a spray bottle with warm water and 10 drops of your favourite essential oil. You can play around and mix a few oils together to achieve your preferred scent.

MAKE YOUR OWN
FABRIC REFRESHER SPRAY

You can make your own fabric refresher spray to refresh your carpets, curtains and fabric surfaces. Half-fill a spray bottle with boiling water, add 2 teaspoons bicarbonate of soda and a few drops of your favourite essential oil, shake to mix and leave for about 30 minutes for the mixture to infuse. Always spray items from a distance of at least 20 cm/8 inches and be careful around pets and children.

CREATE A SPA EXPERIENCE IN YOUR BATHROOM

Dried eucalyptus stems are great for creating a sense of tranquillity in your bathroom. After taking a hot bath or shower, tie a bundle of eucalyptus together, hang it up and the steam in the bathroom will release the plant's oils, creating a fresh, clean smell.

HOMEMADE REED DIFFUSER

I really struggle to find good reed diffusers; even with the expensive ones, I find the smell only really lasts a few days, so I have stopped wasting my money. Instead, I create my own diffuser using water, almond oil, and my favourite essential oils, mixed together in an open-topped glass jar.

HOUSEHOLD PLANTS

Having a few natural plants in your home will purify the air and keep your home smelling fresh and clean. The best ones to look out for are aloe vera and spider plants.

WAX MELTS

I jumped on wax melts last year; I am only sorry that I didn't discover them sooner. They give off an amazing smell and are so much safer to use than candles. If you are yet to treat yourself to an electric wax melt burner, then you must. You can programme them to give off scent at a set time. I tend to have mine on all the time and change the melts every few days.

COOK SOMETHING DELICIOUS

Consider baking bread, a batch of cookies, or banana bread. Toast fresh rosemary in a dry pan or place some cinnamon sticks in your slow cooker. Their scents are amazing.

MAKE A CARPET POWDER

One of the most overlooked spots where unwanted smells accumulate is in the fibres of your carpet. Eliminate these odours by making your own deodorising carpet powder with bicarbonate of soda and your favourite essential oil. Sprinkle the powder onto your carpets, wait for 30 minutes, then vacuum as usual. Not only does the powder help pick up dirt and hair, it also leaves behind a light, fresh scent.

ON THE HOB

Fill a saucepan with water, add some slices of lemon and a few of your favourite herbs, then simmer over a low heat to create a fresh smell and eliminate any cooking odours. Some of my other favourite combinations are:

+ Orange slices, star anise, cinnamon sticks, cloves, 1 tablespoon vanilla extract
+ Rosemary sprigs, lemon slices, 1 tablespoon vanilla extract
+ Cranberries (frozen or fresh), orange slices, nutmeg, cloves, cinnamon sticks
+ Cranberries and cinnamon sticks

COTTON BALL TRICK

Lightly dampen a cotton ball, add 6 drops of your favourite essential oil, then pop this in the bottom of your bin.

How to look after beauty products

Dirty make-up brushes, clogged with old make-up, dust, dirt and oil, can cause skin irritation problems and a break-out of spots or red patches. Make-up brushes do need to be cleaned on a regular basis to stop the build-up of bacteria that is not good for our skin. This is an important task – if you wear make-up daily, make cleaning your brushes a weekly cleaning task.

As well as keeping your make-up brushes clean, keep your make-up bag or storage boxes clean, too. Bacteria love dark places, so make-up containers and bags are the perfect breeding ground. Most make-up bags can go in the wash and boxes should be cleaned out at least once a month. In this way, you can take care of make-up spillages and ensure that all the make-up is in good condition with the lids on and in some sort of order.

TOP TIPS FOR CLEANING MAKE-UP BRUSHES

+ When cleaning your brushes, never soak them. You want to avoid water getting into the handle and harming the glue that holds the brush together.

+ Apply a small amount of baby shampoo or gentle washing-up liquid to the palm of your hand, then swirl the brush around in it, ensuring it gets right into the fibres. If you want to soften and moisturise the bristles, repeat the process using a small amount of hair conditioner.

+ Rinse under cold running water, holding the brush downwards and pulling the product out very gently with your fingertips.

+ Remove any excess water with a clean towel.

+ Lay the brush flat on a clean towel or piece of kitchen paper to dry. Reshape while damp, if you need to.

+ Don't ever stand the brush up to dry. The water will drip into the handle and potentially damage the glue.

+ Don't forget to do this on a regular basis. Brushes can take a few days to get properly dry, so ensure you have plenty of spares to hand.

BATHROOM TOILETRIES AND MAKE-UP DECLUTTERING

How often do you actually check the dates on your bathroom toiletries and make-up? We should get into the habit of checking products to ensure we don't cause ourselves any minor irritations. Set aside time at least twice a year to do a bathroom stock-check. I find January and July are really good times for this (with January comes my new year declutter and with July comes the summer holiday, when the suncreams come out).

+ Put products with a shorter lifespan to the front of your cabinets and ensure you finish them before opening another similar product.
+ You may have products that haven't quite reached their expiry date, but are already gunky. Check each item well for odd textures, smells and colours – if these things have changed, it is time to toss the product.
+ Use mini storage baskets and put them into your bathroom cabinets, labelled, for different types of items, such as 'shampoos' or 'body washes'. This way, you will always know how much you have left of each type of product.
+ Try not to over-buy. Use up what you already have before buying more. This will save a huge build-up of products that can take ages to get through.

Toiletries expiry guide

This is a rough guide – always check a product's shelf-life once opened, which will be printed on the packaging.

HAIR STYLING PRODUCTS	Up to 1–5 years (products containing alcohol tend to last longer)
DEODORANT	Up to 3 years
SHAVING CREAM	Up to 2 years
TOOTHPASTE	Up to 2 years (always check the expiration date, as the product contains fluoride)
MOUTHWASH	Up to 3 years
BODY WASH	Up to 3 years
BODY LOTION	Up to 3 years
FACIAL CLEANSER	Up to 2 years
FACIAL MOISTURISER	Up to 2 years
EYE CREAM	6–12 months, once opened
SUNSCREEN	1 year (this is government regulated)
ANTI-ACNE PRODUCTS	Products containing benzoyl peroxide will only be effective for 3 months; other products can last up to 1 year (depending on ingredients)

ANTI-AGING PRODUCTS	6–12 months (depending on ingredients)
SHAMPOO	1–2 years (opened); up to 3 years (unopened)
CONDITIONER	1–2 years (opened); up to 3 years (unopened)
FOUNDATION	Up to 18 months
MASCARA	Change every 3 months – or immediately if you have suffered an eye infection
LIQUID EYE LINER	Up to 1 year – or replace if you have suffered an eye infection
EYE AND BROW PENCILS	1–3 years (depending on quality). Sharpen before each use to avoid eye infections
LIQUID EYE SHADOW	Up to 1 year
LIPSTICK	2–3 years (depending on quality). Always keep the lid on
LIP GLOSS	2–3 years (depending on quality)
LIP PENCILS	2–3 years (depending on quality)
CREAM BLUSHER	Up to 1 year
POWDER BLUSHER	2–3 years (depending on quality)
BRONZER	2–3 years (depending on quality)

Nifty cleaning tips for pet owners

Owning a pet is a delight – they can bring so much joy into your life, but it isn't always easy! Trust me, I know. Cleaning up after furry friends can sometimes feel like a dull, never-ending task, but it doesn't have to be. The key to being a good pet owner is to be organised.

My family had wanted a dog for a long time and it took me a while to decide whether I could bring a furry friend into my home. But I was sensible and I did my research. For anyone thinking of introducing a pet to their home, I highly recommend borrowing a dog for the day, to see how you feel and how you cope.

Loving your pet is a lot more important than being stressed over muddy paws and shed hair. By following these simple tips you can make life with your pet easier.

DOG CLEANING TIPS

Are you worried your home has developed a doggie smell? Are you ready for fur-free floors and fresh-smelling sofas? Then follow my top tips:

+ Brush your dog daily. It removes those loose hairs before they settle on your sofa and become embedded into your carpet.
+ Invest in plenty of throws for your furniture and wash them regularly.
+ Recycle old bath towels and use them exclusively for your furry friend.
+ Be prepared for after walks. Set up a dog-cleaning station by the door. Keep an old towel and a warm bowl of water nearby, so that when you enter you can dip your dog's paws into it before they have the run of the house.
+ Invest in a barrier mat for all your entrances. These mats are great for absorbing dirt and will help keep your floors clean.

CAT LITTER TRAYS

Cats are – in general – relatively clean, but going the extra mile to keep your home looking spotless is never a bad idea.

Keep litter trays fresh. Line the bottom of the tray with a plastic bag. When it comes to cleaning out the dirty litter tray, there's nothing that makes the job easier and it stops the plastic from absorbing bad smells.

Add a thin layer of bicarbonate of soda to the litter tray before adding kitty litter and it should help keep any smells under control between changes.

PET HAIR

Every pet owner needs to have a lint roller in their cleaning caddy. It's the perfect tool for picking up pet hair, which cannot always be easily sucked up by your vacuum. Simply run the roller over your sofa cushions daily and over any places that your pet likes to settle. You will be amazed at what you can pick up.

Rubber gloves are another great tool for picking up pet hair from your furniture, curtains, cushions and any other fabrics. Pop a pair on, dampen them slightly, then sweep your hands over the hair-ridden areas. Use your fingers to get into those hard to reach areas – hair will quickly stick to the rubber.

PET BEDS

Pet beds can pick up strong odours and they need to be cleaned regularly. Make sure you choose a pet bed with removable covers.

✦ Wash bedding on a hot cycle. Use a mild detergent with no dyes or fragrance and avoid fabric conditioner. By adding a cupful of bicarbonate of soda to the wash, this will help to neutralise any stubborn smells. If you can, save this chore for a sunny day, so that they can dry outside – great for killing bad odours.
✦ Keep a tumble-dryer sheet in an envelope under your pet's bed to keep it smelling fresh.

PET ACCIDENTS

It's something all pet owners dread! A pet accident on the carpet not only looks bad, but the lingering odour can be really hard to get rid of. Act as quickly as you can when an accident occurs. There are many great products you can buy for pet accidents, but I like to use a pet-friendly natural solution. These kitchen staples make an effective stain remover with added odour-neutralising properties:

In a 500 ml spray bottle, mix together a 50:50 solution of white wine vinegar and water and add 4 heaped teaspoons bicarbonate of soda. Bring it out whenever your pet has an accident. First, blot the stain with a cloth, then spray your stain remover liberally on top. Leave for 10 minutes to allow the solution to work, then blot again.

COLLARS AND HARNESSES

Pet collars and harnesses can get grubby and smelly pretty quickly. Don't keep just one set, have a few. The easiest and most effective way to deep clean them is to put a couple of squirts of pet shampoo into a bowl and fill it with hot water. Pop the collars in to soak for at least 15 minutes, then rub them against themselves to extract any dirt. Rinse under a cool tap and pat with a towel before hanging to dry.

PET TOYS

Dishwashers aren't just for cleaning plates, pots and pans. I wash many other items in my dishwasher, including plastic pet toys, to keep them germ free. Fabric toys can be put in the washing machine.

FRESH AIR

I have my windows open all the time. I love fresh air blowing through my house and I feel it wakes my house up every morning. If you own a pet, fresh air is important and will make a huge difference to how your home feels.

How to look after your car interior

I often find that, while people are keen to keep the inside of their homes super-pristine, when it comes to their cars it's a different story. If you have too much rubbish and debris on the floor or on the dashboard, it can get in the way of your driving. You don't want slippy controls or an old water bottle rolling around with the risk of it getting stuck under your pedals. If you don't keep car windows nice and clean, the build-up of dirt and grime can prevent you seeing properly and could potentially cause a nasty accident.

Cleaning the interior of your car is important for maintenance and value. Cleaning the car interior is also something you can get the children involved in, providing it is parked up in a safe area.

DECLUTTER

Start by decluttering your car and make a point of adding this to your family cleaning schedule. Better still, get into the habit of taking any rubbish with you every time you leave the car. Don't leave it in the car to accumulate.

If you have anything in the boot (an old sports bag or a bag of clothes that you have been meaning to drop off at the charity shop), make sure you deal with it. You may also have books, magazines, toys or note pads in the car. The car is not for storage – clear them out regularly.

WIPE DOWN THE INTERIOR FITTINGS

Start with the dashboard, so that any dust or dirt that falls can be vacuumed up later. Take a bowl of clean soapy water and a few old cloths and wipe over the dashboard, door pockets and around the glove box. Don't forget to wipe over the steering wheel and gear stick and any little trays or compartments. A cotton bud is useful for hard-to-reach areas or for cleaning around any electrical buttons.

Buff dry with a clean dry cloth, then use a glass cleaner and give it all a final buff for a shiny finish.

WINDOWS

If you have young children, the car windows may have quite a few sticky finger marks. Microfibre cloths are great for cleaning windows and glass and they avoid streaking. Wipe down with a mixture of white wine vinegar and water and buff dry with a clean cloth.

CAR MATS

Take these out and give them a really good shake. If they are the plastic type, give them a really good clean with warm soapy water and a sponge. Hang them to dry naturally.

If you have carpeted mats, give them a really good vacuum. If they smell, sprinkle with bicarbonate of soda with a nice essential oil mixed in. Leave for about 1 hour, then just vacuum the bicarbonate of soda off.

VACUUM

While the mats are drying, give the car a really good vacuum. Start at the top and work your way down and use the vacuum nozzle attachment. First, give the seats a really good vacuum, including the head rests, and get right into those crevices. Then, tackle the floor and the boot.

SEATS

If you have any stains or marks on the seats, use an upholstery cleaner. If you have leather seats, wash over with warm soapy water and buff dry with a clean cloth. Use a leather treatment to keep them in good condition.

Finish with a good spray of fabric refresher. Give my homemade refresher a try (see page 19) and leave your car smelling really good.

Don't forget to put back your nice clean mats.

It is so satisfying to have a clean car interior. The next time you use it, it will smell lovely and will make your driving experience a whole lot more enjoyable.

Let's talk about plastic

We all need to try to make a few changes to reduce our use of plastic and dispose of it properly. Follow a few of my simple steps to help reduce plastic in your home.

Buy in bulk

Buying cleaning products and food in bulk uses less packaging than buying smaller amounts more frequently. Transfer perishable foods, such as cereals, to air-tight tubs to keep them fresh and it will have the two-fold benefit of helping the environment and saving you money!

Re-use shopping bags

Plastic bags are a big culprit in contributing to our plastic usage, but there are so many alternatives. Take bags with you when you go shopping, carry a lightweight cotton or canvas bag with you at all times or, if you're only buying one or two items, just carry the items yourself.

Make your own cleaning products

Shop-bought cleaning products tend to be made from concentrate and contain up to ninety per cent water. You're essentially paying for water and the plastic bottle. Why not make your own cleaning products using the recipes in this book!

Make home-cooked meals

Avoid ready meals and takeaways packaged in plastic and cook from scratch with fresh ingredients at home. Not only will you reduce your plastic consumption, but it will save you money and improve your diet.

Avoid wet wipes and cleaning wipes

As handy as they are, avoid using cleaning wipes, wet wipes and baby wipes as they are made with plastic resins such as polyester and are responsible for clogging drains when they are flushed down the toilet.

Avoid drinking straws

Plastic straws are an easy one to avoid, especially the ones that come wrapped in plastic — a double whammy! Just sip your beverages right from the cup, or you can use a paper straw or try a reusable one.

Use reusable water bottles

Reusable water bottles are perhaps the easiest way you can reduce your plastic consumption and there are so many options available, in so many styles and materials. I never leave home without mine.

Replace your razor blades

Replace disposable plastic razors with a metal razor that will take replaceable razor blades.

STAYING
ON TOP
OF THE MESS

☆ Organisation and planning

In my experience, the best ways to get the most out of your cleaning and be as efficient as possible are preparation and organisation.

Motivation

Getting motivated to clean does not come easy for many of us. Sometimes, we can get so overwhelmed with the mess that we really don't know where to start. These simple steps will help activate you. It doesn't matter whether you are looking to clean one room or an entire house, these tips will give you the drive to tackle any task at hand.

THE CLEANING CALENDAR

It's important to have some sort of plan in place. I have created a monthly cleaning calendar with daily tasks to keep you on top of your housework (see pages 132-133). Follow the calendar or even create your own and you will find that you get into such a good routine that the cleaning becomes easy. It's the perfect tool for anyone feeling lost with their housework and it will really help start the motivation process.

BE STRUCTURED

Choose a time of the day when you feel at your best and fully motivated and keep to cleaning at this time of day when you can. I'm an early riser and love to get all my cleaning and household chores done first thing in the morning, so I have the rest of the day to enjoy. You may choose to come home from work at lunchtimes and have a quick tidy up when the house is empty, or you may prefer to do your cleaning in the evening. However, whatever you choose, you must stick to a structure.

KNOW YOUR HOME

This may sound silly, but really get to know your home. Work out where those 'WA's (worst areas) are and give these areas extra time and focus.

+ Where are the high-traffic areas?
+ Where do you find the dust settles the most?
+ Where do all the bits and bobs end up?

REMOVE DISTRACTIONS

This is easier said than done, but there are a few things you can do right now to stop the distractions that can crop up when you are tidying and cleaning.

+ Set your phone to 'do not disturb' while you are cleaning – a phone constantly beeping at you with social media alerts and text messages isn't going to help.
+ You don't need the constant distractions that kids can create. Try to do your cleaning when they are at school or doing their homework or, if you have younger children, during nap time.

LISTEN TO MUSIC

I find music helps you clean faster and keeps you focused and on track. Choose some fast-paced happy music to clean to. Make yourself a different playlist for each day of the week and listen to it when you're tidying and cleaning.

Music helps keep you motivated and makes you move your body more, which, in turn, transforms your cleaning into a little work-out. Speed cleaning is just as good as any gym workout. Cleaning makes you work every part of your body and the faster the work is, the better it is for you (see pages 176-177).

MY 5-MINUTE CLEANING CHALLENGE

For quick tidy-up and cleaning sessions, my most simple and effective cleaning method is to set a timer. When you walk into a room and see all the mess, it can be worrying – you think to yourself 'how on earth will I get all that done?' The timer will give you encouragement and focus.

Set the timer on your phone, oven or clock to 5 minutes. Start at the room entrance, press 'start' and see how much you can get done against the clock. Rather like a game, you are setting yourself a personal challenge. Now, 5 minutes might seem like very little time. I mean, in that time you can probably just scroll through social media, send a quick email or a few texts… but 5 minutes used wisely is actually quite a long time. When the timer goes off, stand back and see what you have achieved. Trust me, you will be surprised.

Quick Room-by-Room Cleaning Schedule
(to take no more than 5 minutes per room)

Bathrooms	Bedrooms	Kitchen	Lounge
Clean the sink with a quick spray and a wipe around with a cloth.	Make the bed and spray with a deodoriser.	Wipe down surfaces with a multipurpose spray.	Plump sofa cushions and spray with a fabric refresher.
Wipe the toilet seat and the rim and add toilet cleaner or bleach.	Tidy up any clothes that haven't been put away.	Wipe any floor spillages and the top of the bin with the same cloth.	Tidy up coffee tables.
Polish the mirrors.	Straighten the dressing table.	Clean the sink and buff dry, so it looks nice and shiny.	Quick vacuum.
Squeegee the shower door and tiles.	Plump cushions on the bed and bedroom chairs.	Pop used tea towels and cloths in the washing machine.	Quick polish.
Shake bath mats out.	Put TV remote controls in the drawer.		
Leave the window open to air.	Pull open the curtains and blinds.		
	Leave the window slightly open to air.		

Take the bedroom; in 5 minutes you can:

+ Open the curtains
+ Open the window
+ Make the bed
+ Put away any clothes that are lying around

Okay, you haven't given your bedroom a deep clean, but you have made a start. If you then go off to work or the school run, you aren't leaving your room in a real mess.

Let's look at the kitchen; what can you achieve in 5 minutes:

+ Empty the dishwasher
+ Spray and clean the surfaces
+ Run the vacuum around

So, if you wanted to invite a friend back for a cuppa and catch up after the school run, you could do so without feeling embarrassed.

The timer motivates you and makes you want to achieve. I tend to advise people who have a busy life and very little time for housework to give this a try. Choose the rooms that are lived in the most and that you want to see tidy. Set the timer and go!

Timers don't just come in the form of a clock

Think about the mornings when you get up tired and go into the kitchen to make a cup of tea or coffee. While the kettle is boiling, what do you actually do? Do you just stand there? Do you scroll through social media? Why not use this time wisely instead? A full kettle takes roughly 3 minutes to boil. Use the time to do something productive. Why not:

+ Empty the dishwasher
+ Do a pile of washing up
+ Start to make the kids' packed lunches
+ Empty the washing machine
+ Fold some laundry
+ Write a to-do list
+ Declutter and tidy a kitchen drawer
+ Sort through your handbag
+ Wipe over an appliance
+ Clean the kitchen window

There is so much you can do in this short amount of time that can make a difference to your whole day. Next time you boil the kettle or put something in the microwave to defrost, I want you to think about this and try it.

Routine

Keeping a house tidy all the time can be daunting and is not especially easy if you have a large family who bring in plenty of clutter and are hard to clean up after. However, if we don't tackle those piles of clutter or small cleaning jobs regularly, they soon build up and become an enormous job that our busy lives don't allow us time to tackle. It is so important to stick to a routine to enable your family ship to sail.

MOTIVATIONAL HASHTAGS

If you follow me on social media then you know that I use a daily hashtag system to help get people motivated and to share the cleaning buzz. When you see someone cleaning, you naturally start to clean yourself. I noticed that when I was on Obsessive Compulsive Cleaners, which was aired at 8pm. At 9pm I would get loads of messages saying 'because of you and the show I am now cleaning at 9pm at night'. Cleaning is one of those things that does have a positive knock-on effect.

I put together a hashtag system to continue creating this buzz and to motivate – it works so well. If you want to follow along with the hashtags but don't use social media then why not set these as daily alarms on your phone (set them so that you get more than one reminder a day and it will help you get into a routine).

Monday: #motivationalmonday

On Monday mornings, we are all feeling a little gloomy – a new week has just started and we are tired after the weekend, so it's important to share some motivation. Text a friend and send them a picture of you doing some housework. A 10-minute cleaning session will wake you up and set you up for the day.

Tuesday: #toilettuesday

Now, toilets are something that I recommend you clean every day, especially the downstairs WC as this is often the highest traffic toilet in your home. On Tuesday I want you to scrub your toilet. Get on your hands and knees and give the base of the toilet a really good scrub. Take a toothbrush and go around where the screws are, then thoroughly wipe the seat over. Finish off with a nice big squirt of bleach. You don't need to do this every time you clean the toilet, but #toilettuesday is all about that deep clean.

TOILET TIP

If you have a handheld steamer, give toilets a weekly steam to kill all those germs.

Wednesday: #windowswednesday

Internal window cleaning is not an enjoyable task. So, I suggest just doing a few at a time – they don't all need doing every week. Focus on the high-traffic windows, where hand prints and pet marks often appear, but for the rest create a monthly pattern. For example, do the downstairs windows one week, then upstairs the following week. Don't just clean the glass, make sure you also focus on the frames. If you have PVC frames, use a cream cleaner to keep the PVC nice and bright.

Thursday: #throwitthursday

We need to do a little decluttering on a weekly basis. Do you find you have an area in your home where the paperwork builds up and that there are always general bits and pieces hanging around that need putting away? Grab a standard-size carrier bag and make a point of filling it up on a Thursday to get rid of that clutter. Don't forget to recycle.

FRIDGE TIP

Use a damp cotton bud with a little washing-up liquid to clean the rubber seal.

Friday: #fridgefriday

I have always thought that fridges don't get enough attention. Fridges look after our food, but do we look after our fridges? Use Fridays to empty out the fridge and check over your food items. Check the best-before and use-by dates and throw out what you need to. Give the fridge a good wipe over and, if you have any nasty fridge odours, place a dish of bicarbonate of soda towards the back to soak up those smells. You will probably find that by giving your fridge a weekly clean, odours will soon become a thing of the past.

Saturday: #stairssaturday

Vacuuming stairs is another one of those cleaning tasks that we put off and off. The thought of lugging a big vacuum up the stairs is just not good. But they need doing. Stairs take a lot of traffic and, if we don't vacuum them on a regular basis, our carpets will start to look old and worn out. Invest in a lighter handheld vacuum for the stairs.

BEDDING TIP

Find the best washing combination of detergent and fabric conditioner so your bed smells amazing. Add a few drops of lavender essential oil to your mattress to help improve your sleep.

Sunday: #cleansheetssunday

There is nothing better than climbing into fresh-smelling ironed sheets on a Sunday night. Clean sheets really help aid a good night's sleep and it's the best way to start a new week. Create a little pattern to rotating your bedding: e.g. clean the mattress and pillow protectors every other wash. Give your mattress a little vacuum, too.

My monthly cleaning calendar

1	2	3	4	5	6	7
Wash or steam floors.	Change towels and bedding.	Wipe over kitchen bins, bathroom bins and clean fridge doors.	Wipe down front door and tidy up outside.	Clean internal windows and mirrors and wash or steam floors.	Full fridge clean and do the ironing.	Bathroom full clean and towel and mat change.
8	**9**	**10**	**11**	**12**	**13**	**14**
Wash internal walls down and wash or steam floors.	Clean washing machine, change towels and bedding and turn mattress.	Full kitchen clean, including dishwasher, tops of cupboards and inside drawers.	Furniture polish and clean blinds or put net curtains in the wash.	Wash or steam floors and put cushion covers in the wash.	Clean oven and do the ironing.	Bathroom full clean and change mats and towels.
15	**16**	**17**	**18**	**19**	**20**	**21**
Wipe and clean internal doors and clean light switches.	Wash floors and wipe bins and fridge; change towels and bedding.	Clean internal windows and mirrors.	Clear out cupboards and do the ironing.	Get up high for cobwebs and clean the banisters and clean carpets.	Wash or steam floors and clean fridge.	Full bathroom clean and change towels and mats and clean kitchen.
22	**23**	**24**	**25**	**26**	**27**	**28**
Vacuum sofas and pull them out.	Wash or steam floors and polish furniture.	Wash out the bins and change bedding and towels.	Clean oven and do the ironing.	Wipe down kitchen chairs and leather sofas.	Full kitchen clean, including tops of cupboards and wash floors.	Full bathroom clean, clear out cupboards; change towels and bedding.
29	**30**	**31**				
Bedding change and hoover and steam mattress.	Clean outside bins and front and back doors.	Wash or steam floors.				

EXTRA CLEANING TASKS
(for when you have time)

✦ Vacuum skirting boards ✦ Dust light fixtures
✦ Treat wooden furniture ✦ Wash/fluff pillows and bedding ✦ Turn/rotate/vacuum mattress

Have a go at creating
your own monthly cleaning calendar here

1	2	3	4	5	6	7
8	9	10	11	12	13	14
15	16	17	18	19	20	21
22	23	24	25	26	27	28
29	30	31				

EXTRA CLEANING TASKS

The daily to-do list

Get time back in your day with a to-do list.

I always find that keeping things in your head creates a sense of panic and anxiety. When you are juggling lots of tasks, they can seem overwhelming, especially with the added worry of forgetting something. So for me, no morning is complete without a to-do list. It includes everything from going to the shops to stock up on bread and milk, to work emails and calls, housework, meal preparation and general family organisation. Anything and everything that needs to be done gets written down – even to the tiniest detail of who I need to text that day!

TRACK YOUR PROGRESS

A to-do list means you can mark off the tasks you have completed. At the end of the day, when you look at the list, it will give you a wonderful sense of accomplishment and satisfaction. Alternatively, it might give you the push you need to complete your day if you haven't finished what you needed to! It might also have the effect of a wake-up call if nothing has been marked as completed.

BE REALISTIC

Make sure you don't include more on your list than you can accomplish within a day. Projects that will take weeks or months to complete should be organised and tracked in a different way. The to-do list is purely to help manage your day.

MONTHLY LISTS

Regular tasks can occur on a monthly cycle. Create a monthly list that will remind you to complete tasks that are regular, but not frequent. A calendar is the easiest place to track such a list.

The weekly deep clean

Together with my husband, I deep clean the house on Sunday mornings. Housework is all about team work and so we set aside this time each week to give the house a really thorough clean. While I love doing my 5-minute cleaning challenge in the week, when I am busy with work and school, this doesn't give the home a deep clean – it's more of a freshen up and tidy to restore order. I highly recommend you set aside some time for a weekly or fortnightly deep clean and really focus on those high-traffic areas and worst areas.

A deep clean includes:
+ Cleaning behind and under the sofa
+ Refreshing sofa cushions with the vacuum
+ Removal of cobwebs with a high-reach duster
+ Dusting internal doors
+ Dusting skirting boards
+ Wiping over radiators
+ Damp wipe of light switches and sockets
+ Damp wipe of door handles

CLEANING YOUR CLEANING APPLIANCES

When you're deep cleaning, it's time to think about your appliances. Those things that clean for you need a bit of a clean, too. These simple little tasks will keep your appliances running better and ensure that you are actually cleaning your home effectively.

+ Your washing machine needs a little TLC – if your machine isn't clean, your clothes won't be clean. Make a point of running an empty hot wash with white wine vinegar. Remove the detergent dispenser drawer and wash it to remove any soap and grime build-up.
+ Give your vacuum a little consideration. Empty it. Take apart the bits you can and give them a little rinse using warm soapy water. Wipe over the wheels and clean the brush bar.
+ Run an empty hot wash on your dishwasher, with a little added lemon juice.

Mental and bodily health benefits of a clean and tidy home

I am a firm believer in the saying 'a clean house is a happy house'. If you can maintain a clean and organised home you will bring a sense of accomplishment, happiness, serenity and clarity to your home.

I have cleaned many houses that are very badly disorganised and unclean. The relief clients feel when I have helped restore order is unbelievable. I see their faces light up and we often find a whole host of missing belongings, too. Neatness and order *do* support our health and wellbeing.

Reduce stress

When you live in an untidy environment, your stress levels will naturally be higher, you will be disorganised, and you will find it hard to find certain items. Living in a clean and organised home will give you a healthier lifestyle: you will be able to prepare healthy meals in your kitchen, sleep well in your bedroom and you will become more active. It's pretty amazing what a healthy, clean home can do to lift your spirits, too.

Increase productivity

Without dirt and clutter your mind becomes free to focus on everything else in life.

Relieve tension

An organised house will relieve tension between you and other family members. When everything has its place, there will be less arguing – everyone will know where everything is.

Encourage creativity

A clean and tidy home will give you space to think. You will have plenty of room to implement changes and come up with great ideas for storage solutions and decorative schemes.

Discourage germs

You will lessen the spread of germs and bacteria, resulting in a healthier lifestyle. Every time you clean the house with disinfectants, you are killing bacteria, viruses and other microorganisms that can compromise your health.

Alleviate allergies

If you have family members that suffer with allergies or asthma, a clean and tidy home can really help reduce these symptoms. Dust mites, pet dander, mould and mildew can all trigger allergic reactions, compromise air quality and increase potential problems.

Improve safety

Particularly when you have little ones, a clean organised home improves personal safety. You don't want cluttered floors that result in accidents. Sharp objects need to be kept in the correct places. If there are stacks of boxes and other large piles, these can easily fall on top of someone and injure them.

Deter pests

One of the worst symptoms of an unclean and cluttered home is the increase in pest activity. Ants, rats, mice, cockroaches, termites, bed bugs and other household pests are attracted to warm, damp places. Consistent and regular cleaning can deter a lot of potentially hazardous pest problems.

Getting the family involved

A FAMILY THAT CLEANS TOGETHER STAYS TOGETHER!

I live in a busy house with a number of kids and a dog – it's so important that the daily cleaning tasks aren't just the responsibility of one person. Families need to work together and everyone needs to get stuck in with the household chores. If the tasks aren't shared, it's often too much for one person to juggle work with the children and the household chores. If you feel that the burden of housework falls on you alone, then it is time to spread the load.

FAMILY MEETING

Start by calling a family meeting and plan a cleaning schedule that suits everyone. This may be slightly uncomfortable for those that are really reluctant to clean. If you want your family members to take you seriously and get on board, then don't start off by being too harsh with them. Tell them what you expect of them and ask them what they expect of you.

Guide them

If you need to, state a few facts. Compile a list if necessary and ask your family members a few leading questions:

+ Are there always clothes ready on demand?
+ Are the bins emptied?
+ Is the bathroom replenished with toiletries and kept clean?
+ Are the bath mats and towels regularly changed?
+ Is the food cupboard stocked with everyone's favourite snacks?

Make them aware that these tasks are done for them and who by. Explain that it is now time for these tasks to be delegated and shared.

Now, I am not expecting you to suggest to your 5-year-old child that they are responsible for emptying the bin, but you should expect them to do something. Below are some lists of tasks that I feel are suitable for various ages and will give them some responsibilities within the home. Make sure that all the adults that live in the home are doing their bit – if you want your children to clean up their act, you need to ensure all the adults clean up theirs…

CHILDREN AND CHORES

Children can learn a lot from doing household chores. Doing chores helps children learn about what they need to do to care for themselves, a home and a family. It teaches them skills they can use in their adult lives, such as preparing meals, cleaning, organising and keeping a garden. When children contribute to family life, it helps them feel competent and responsible. Even if they don't enjoy the chore, if they keep going they will get the feeling of satisfaction that comes with finishing a task.

One of the easiest and sneakiest ways to get your younger kids excited about cleaning is to turn it into a game. Give them a plastic tub each or a bag and see how quickly they can pick up the toys that are all over the floor. Whoever picks up the most pieces is the winner. Even though they think they are the winner and will be feeling super-proud, you are the real winner here!

Tasks for toddlers

+ Pick up toys and books
+ Hang clothes on clothes hooks
+ Put dirty clothes in the laundry bin
+ Set placemats on the dinner table
+ Hand out the pegs when you are putting the washing on the line

Tasks for primary school-age children

+ Water the garden and indoor plants
+ Feed pets
+ Rinse the bathroom sink after using
+ Empty the tumble dryer
+ Empty the dishwasher
+ Help hang out clothes and fold washing
+ Put away crockery and cutlery
+ Plump sofa cushions
+ Draw the curtains
+ Make their bed daily or pull back the sheets to let their bed air
+ Strip their bedding ready for the wash
+ Help with choosing meals and shopping
+ Help with meal preparation and serving (with supervision)

Tip

Organise uniform for the week ahead. Take a few minutes every Sunday evening to lay out and organise the uniform for the coming week. Match together five complete outfits and hang them on one hanger each. Label the hangers with the days of the week. This will enable your child to take out their daily outfit and saves you having to do this in the hectic mornings.

CLEANING AND TEENAGERS

It can feel impossible to get your teenagers to help around the house, but it just takes patience. One of the biggest conflicts in the family home with teenagers is often about cleaning. Teens get sick of being nagged and will leave that wet towel on the bathroom floor and their coat thrown on the sofa. However, they need to learn that this is not how to behave and that when they move out of home, they simply won't be able to live like this.

It is important to raise a clean teen

Parents do need to respect teenagers' need for independence and privacy, but teenagers also need to respect their parents and follow some ground rules. After all, they live in your home where the majority of tasks are done for them.

Tasks for teens

These tasks are basic but it gets them up and moving, off their phones, out of their rooms, and interacting with the family:

+ Helping with dinner
+ Doing some grocery shopping
+ Stripping and washing their own bedding
+ Emptying bins and rinsing bins out
+ Vacuuming
+ Loading the dishwasher
+ Washing up
+ Cleaning the car inside and out
+ Sorting their laundry into whites and colours
+ Decluttering their wardrobes every now and then

How do you handle them if they don't help support the family home? Many teenagers will probably start off really well, but slip back into their usual lazy habits. If we allowed ourselves to slip back into bad habits, the household ship would sink, so you need to keep reiterating this to them. They can't just give up; the ship does need to sail.

Have sensible consequences

Don't go mad and end up having a huge argument with them. Choose a sensible and proportional punishment. Remember, they live under your roof and rules do need to be adhered to.

+ If you give them an allowance, mention docking it
+ Set an earlier curfew for when they go out and about
+ Possibly threaten the dreaded 'I am going to take your phone off you' (you are probably the one paying the bill, so you're quite within your rights to do this)

If this still doesn't work, play your trump card. Casually explain that, if they won't play ball, you have no choice but to hire a cleaner and you will use their phone money or allowance to pay for it. Bingo! They won't want a stranger in their room, moving their stuff. Argument won…

Design a family rota

Before you design your rota, a chore list needs to be put together. Categorise cleaning tasks according to weekly and daily priorities (see pages 132-133 for examples).

1   Make a list of cleaning tasks.

2   Separate them into weekly and daily tasks.

3   Decide who does what.

4   Create a reward chart for the younger family members.

5   Pick a time that suits everyone (e.g. you may choose a Sunday afternoon).

6   Mix the jobs up a bit to make it more fun.

7   Set a timer – make it a bit of a competition.

A family rota is going to evolve and get better over time. You may assign tasks to a family member and realise that it's just not right for them or is taking much longer than it should. Be patient with the rota, design it together and tweak if needed. Do not put too much pressure on everyone.

'WA's (WORST AREAS)

When designing your family rota think of the 'WA's (worst areas). The WA's are those cluttered cupboards, the oven, the tops of kitchen cupboards and under beds. Add the WAs into the rota at least once a month and make sure someone take responsibility for them. For example, everyone that sleeps in a bed needs to be responsible for what is underneath it (that missing sock, plate, bits of tissue, odd coins, dirty laundry and so on). The underneath of a bed is not a storage area.

DAY	TASKS	FAMILY MEMBER
SUNDAY		
MONDAY		
TUESDAY		
WEDNESDAY		
THURSDAY		
FRIDAY		
SATURDAY		

DON'T PANIC!

Tips for the worst cleaning challenges

☆

Here is my guide to what to do in a cleaning emergency.

The stainbuster guide

Stains – we all get them. For those of us with young children, clothing and carpet stains can be an everyday occurrence. The key to dealing with stains is not to panic and to get to them as soon as possible.

When out and about (especially if you know you are going to be out for most of the day), carry some hand sanitiser gel with you, as it's really good for quick fixes. I carry a handy little cleaning kit around with me, containing a mini multipurpose cleaner, hand sanitiser, hand soap and tissues, so I am always quick to respond to sticky coffee tables and spillages.

Most stains can be dealt with very easily. Here are a few of my favourite simple, yet effective, treatments to banish stains quickly:

Tip

Always use a white cloth to tackle stains, as this allows you to see how much of the stain you are actually removing.

SPILT COFFEE ON CLOTHING

Sponge off straight away with cold (NOT HOT) water. Dab the stain – do not rub or you will spread it even further.

If you are out and about, your hand sanitiser gel can act as an instant stain remover, if you get to it quickly.

Once home, turn your stained clothing inside out and hold under cold runnning water, letting the water flush the stain through the fibres. Turn back the right way and rinse again under warm water. Rub in a little washing-up liquid and then leave for 30 minutes. Rinse and wash as normal.

RED WINE ON CARPET

Wine spillages at dinner parties are a common occurrence. Take a white cloth, place it over the stain and allow it to soak up any excess wine that hasn't yet soaked into the carpet. Half-fill a washing-up bowl with warm water, add one squirt of washing-up liquid and a drop of white wine vinegar and scrub the mixture into the stain. Leave to work for a few minutes, then use a white cloth to blot dry.

VOMIT

We've all been there – whether it's from a human or a pet, it's not easy cleaning up vomit from carpets and you need to have a strong stomach. First, use a blunt knife to scrape up as much as you can (not very pleasant, I know!). Using a sieve, sprinkle over a good dose of bicarbonate of soda (bicarb is great for soaking up sick smells). Leave it to work for 15 minutes, then vacuum it up. Using warm water with a dash of white vinegar, scrub the stain clean. Blot dry. If the smell persists, repeat the process using the bicarb, with an added drop of your favourite essential oil, too, if wished.

INK

Ever had a pen leak in your pocket or do your kids come back from school with their shirts covered in ink marks? Ink isn't an easy stain to tackle. The key to this stain is rubbing alcohol – the type used for cleaning minor cuts, abrasions and burns, which can be found in most chemists. I highly recommend keeping a bottle of this in your cleaning caddy. Submerge the stain in the alcohol for 15 minutes, then rinse under cold running water. Apply a prewash treatment, then wash as normal. Check the stain has gone before you pop anything into the tumble dryer – the heat from the dryer will further fix the stain into the fabric.

GRASS

This is one of the easier stains to remove. Simply rub a little neat biological laundry detergent into the stain (a toothbrush is really good for this, as it will help loosen it). Leave to work for 15 minutes, then wash as normal.

CHOCOLATE

Have you ever sat on a chocolate and ended up with a great big stain on your trousers? I know I have and it can be rather embarrassing. Take a blunt knife and scrape away any excess chocolate, flush under cold running water, then rub in some biological laundry detergent. Leave for 15 minutes, then wash as normal.

BLOOD

The sooner you act, the better – getting rid of dried-in blood stains is not easy. Turn the garment inside-out and flush under cold running water (DO NOT use hot water, as this will embed the stain even further into the fabric). Apply some neat white vinegar to the stain and leave for 30 minutes, then wash as normal.

GREASE AND OIL

Forget to put on your apron when cooking? Covered in splash marks from cooking up a tasty steak? Grease and oil stains can get everywhere – try to get to the stain as soon as possible. Squeeze over some fresh or bottled lemon juice to cover the stain. Then, take some table salt, sprinkle onto the stain and rub it in. Leave for a few minutes, then rinse with warm water and wash as normal.

NAIL POLISH

When painting our nails we can occasionally get nail polish on the furniture – usually an acetone nail polish remover will remove this easily. However, if you spill some onto the carpet, it is a different story. The go-to product for this type of spillage is window cleaner. Apply direct to the stain and use circular motions with a white cloth to remove it. Rinse with warm water and repeat, if necessary.

PAINT

Paint is a relatively easy stain to tackle and will normally come out with ease using washing-up liquid. Rub neat into the stain and leave for 30 minutes or so. Rinse and then wash as normal. Repeat the process, if necessary.

FOOD

Bolognese sauce, ketchup or brown sauce are all very noticeable stains that can be awkward to get out. First, rinse with cold water, then turn the garment inside-out and flush the stain under the tap. After flushing, apply neat white wine vinegar and leave for a while. Rinse and wash as normal. Try to get to these stains as soon as possible. DO NOT use hot water as this will help set the stain and make it harder to remove.

CANDLE WAX ON CARPET

A common problem, particularly in the winter months. Use part of a paper bag or an old tea towel to cover the area, then apply gentle heat with a hair dryer or an iron (you don't want it so hot it damages your carpet) and allow the wax to slowly lift off. You may need to repeat this a few times.

Spring cleaning: a step-by-step guide ☆

The annual spring clean could quite possibly be my favourite time of the year! I think spring cleaning should be celebrated and not dreaded – it's time to really refresh our homes and bring them back to life, after those grey days and dark nights when we have spent a lot of time indoors curled up on the sofa, snacking and watching endless amount of television. It's time to pull on those marigolds, dust off those aprons and get cleaning and organising your home.

Spring cleaning is not just about cleaning – it's also about decluttering. It's time to get rid of the unwanted items and rubbish that has accumulated over the year.

Let's get started ...

First, you need to want to do this – see it as a positive task.

Second, you need to be structured:

✦ Set aside a few days to tackle the spring clean.
✦ Put together a checklist of tasks that need to be completed.
✦ Design yourself a fun, fast-paced music playlist.

You will need:

✦ Rubber gloves
✦ Apron
✦ Old clothes
✦ Washing-up bowl or bucket
✦ Microfibre cloths
✦ Sponges
✦ Toothbrush
✦ Floor mop or steamer
✦ Carpet cleaner or vacuum

GENERAL TASKS FOR ALL ROOMS

✦ Disinfect all door and cabinet handles and knobs, using a product spray and a damp cloth.
✦ Wipe over all light switches.
✦ Test batteries in smoke alarms, door bells, etc.
✦ Replace any light bulbs that aren't working.
✦ Open the windows when using chemicals to clean.

THE KITCHEN

Cupboards

Begin with the cupboards. Remove all items and check the use-by dates – if anything is out of date, chuck it away.

Clean the cupboards inside and out, paying attention to the handles, too. Use a good multipurpose cleaner. If you have high-gloss cupboard doors, give these a really good buff (to maintain shine and get rid of any streaks, use a little glass cleaner). If you have wooden doors, use a bit of furniture polish to get them nice and shiny.

Make sure you get a ladder out and do the tops of the cupboards – dust really settles here and with the added cooking fats and greases that accumulate in a kitchen, it can also be rather sticky. Give them a really good clean with warm soapy water and don't forget the top of the extractor fan, too!

Fridge

Now move on to the fridge. Empty it out and, again, look at the use-by dates. Throw away out-of-date, mouldy or unwanted food.

Take out any of the shelves and trays that are removable and put them to soak in warm soapy water.

Meanwhile, clean the rest of the fridge with warm soapy water. If you have any sticky patches, sprinkle with some bicarbonate of soda and leave it for a while to soak in (this will pull the stain up and remove any nasty fridge smells).

Rinse and wipe down the shelves and trays with a microfibre cloth and replace.

If you are strong enough or if you have a helper, pull the fridge out while it's empty and give the floor underneath and the sides a good clean. Dirt really builds up under the fridge and you may even find odd bits of food that have started to smell unpleasant. Don't forget to the clean the top.

Dishwasher
Pour some neat lemon juice into the compartment where you would put the detergent and run empty, on the hottest cycle.

Empty out the filters and give them a really good rinse. Grime and grease can build up here and you may also find traces of old food.

Washing machine
Remove the detergent dispenser drawer and put it to soak in some warm soapy water. If there is any mould or mildew present, add 4 teaspoons white wine vinegar to the soaking water.

Wash the area around where the tray fits into the machine with warm soapy water.

Make a paste of some bicarbonate of soda and lemon juice and use a toothbrush to apply it to and scrub in between the rubber seal and on the drum. Leave for 15 minutes, then wipe away with a damp cloth or pop your machine on for a quick empty cycle.

Make sure you also wipe the outside of the appliance. If you can move it, take it out and clean the floor underneath and the sides.

Oven

To keep your oven clean, you should give it a good wipe down after every single use, but we sometimes forget or don't have the time and grease can build up.

Remove all the shelves or racks, soak them in water and spray them with a good oven cleaning product. Leave for 15 minutes, then clean using some wire wool. For a more natural clean, make a paste with bicarbonate of soda and white wine vinegar, rub it all over, leave for 15 minutes, then rinse.

Meanwhile, spray the oven cleaning product very liberally into the interior of the oven. If the oven is very dirty, leave the product on to soak for a few hours and come back to it when any grime should be easier to remove. Use a scourer pad to clean off the cooked-on grease and pay particular attention to the glass door. If you prefer not to use a chemical product, sprinkle the oven with bicarbonate of soda and spray with vinegar (this will really fizz and lift off the dirt) and then scrub away.

Table and chairs

Wash down any chairs, paying attention to the legs and the feet, then do the same with the table. It's not just the tabletop we need to be worried about – food spills and splashes will also be present on table and chair legs.

Floor

Remove any furniture. Lift chairs or bar stools onto the table, so you don't miss any areas. Pick up any door mats or rugs, shake them outside and leave them outside to air. Give the entire floor a thorough mop.

Fruit bowl

Empty the fruit bowl and soak. This can easily be forgotten, but sticky juices from old fruit can encourage mould growth, which can contaminate your fresh fruit.

BATHROOMS

If you give your bathroom and toilets a good clean a couple of times a week, these rooms should be easy to spring clean.

+ Gather up all the towels, bath mats and flannels and get these in the wash. If any are looking worn or discoloured, then replace.
+ Invest in new toothbrushes or electric toothbrush heads. It's important that these are changed every 3 months, if not more often, if you can. Always remember to keep toothbrushes a good distance away from your toilet, and put the lid down on the toilet before you flush (fine particles of toilet water spray out each time you flush and you don't want them on your toothbrushes!).
+ Go through your medicine cabinet and toiletries and check the dates (see also pages 106-107). If you don't plan to use them or if any are unwanted gifts, then now is the time to get rid of

them. No need to hoard. These can be really useful items to donate to some charities, including the womens' refuge.

+ Use a plunger on the bath and the sinks to ensure drains aren't getting blocked.

+ Use a thin unused mascara brush to get down the plug holes and remove clumps of hair and soap scum build-up.

+ Use a good generic bathroom cleaner that you know will work on all materials in your bathroom, from the tiles to the sink, and a good limescale remover for areas with water marks.

+ Use a toothbrush to clean around the taps and in small gaps.

+ Use a white wine vinegar spray on the taps and in the shower area, then buff with a soft dry cloth to leave a nice gleaming shine.

Tips

Natural cleaning methods for the bathroom:

+ A halved lemon rubbed over the shower screen will bring it up like new, cutting through soap scum and water marks.

+ White wine vinegar is great for deodorising and killing germs.

WINDOWS

Having clean windows can make such a difference to your home. With the right cleaning tools, you can get crystal-clean windows in no time at all.

Before you start, brush off any dust and cobwebs from the windows with a long-handled duster brush. If you are cleaning the exterior of the windows, there may be leaves or insects to deal with, too.

Use hot soapy water to clean the frames inside and out. I just pop a squeeze of washing-up liquid into a bowl of warm water. Next, go over the window glass with a fresh bowl of soapy water. Dry off with a clean dry cloth and finally use a window-cleaning product to finish.

Tips

+ Clean the windows on a cloudy day, so the sun doesn't dry the window-cleaning product onto the glass before you have had a chance to dry them. This avoids smear marks.

+ When drying windows, always wipe horizontally.

+ If you have PVC window frames, a cream cleaner is really good for brightening up the white.

CARPET CLEANING

It's important to look after your carpets; by cleaning them a few times a year, you will be helping to prolong their life in your home.

- Invest in a carpet cleaner to get your carpets smelling and looking fresh again – or you can hire one.
- When using a carpet cleaner, move as much furniture as you can and try to make maximum use of it.
- Open the windows and let your carpet dry naturally to leave your home smelling fresh.

WALLS

I always clean my walls, but many of us don't. Pay particular care to the hallway, as when people enter the house they tend to touch the walls when balancing to take off their shoes.

Start by vacuuming the walls with the brush attachment. Reach as high up as you can to remove all the dust.

HANDY HINT

For stubborn marks, use a new tennis ball. Lightly dampen and gently rub onto the wall to remove unwanted stains and marks.

Get a bowl of warm water and add a squeeze of washing-up liquid and a capful of washing detergent. Use a cloth to gently wipe down the walls with the solution. Don't rub too hard – you don't want to ruin the paintwork or wallpaper.

No need to wipe down. Open the windows and the walls will dry quickly.

LOUNGE/SITTING ROOM

My own lounge has very little in it and not much clutter at all, making it one of the easiest rooms in the home to clean.

+ Start with the sofa and chairs, giving them a really good vacuum. Take all the cushions off and get to the base of the sofa. Afterwards, spray with a fabric refresher.
+ If you have throw cushions or removable covers on the sofa and chairs, remove them and pop them in the washing machine. Don't forget to add your favourite fabric conditioner to keep them smelling good.
+ Pull the sofa out from its position and wash the wall behind it. Wash or vacuum the floor underneath it (if this hasn't been done in a while, you will have a build-up of dust).
+ Clean all the skirting boards.
+ Using your vacuum nozzle, vacuum your blinds and curtains. If you have slatted Venetian blinds, a tumble dryer sheet is great for lifting off the dust.
+ If you have a bookcase or DVD shelving system, take all the items off and look through for anything that you no longer require. Pop unwanted items aside to donate to charity. Give the unit a good clean with a damp cloth (furniture polish alone is not enough to tackle dust build-up), then dry off with a clean dry cloth. When dry, use a furniture polish to give it a shine and a fresh smell.
+ Look through magazine or paper racks and dispose of any old or outdated reading material. Use this opportunity to start afresh with your magazine reading. If you collect magazines, pop them in magazine storage boxes in date order.
+ If you have a rug, soak up any bad smells by using a sieve to

sprinkle some bicarbonate of soda mixed with an essential oil all over it, then vacuum it up. Alternatively, if you have hired a carpet cleaner, use this to freshen it up. You could also go back to the good old-fashioned method of hanging the rug outside in the fresh air and beating it with a big stick. (I have done this a few times and, even though I vacuum my rug at least twice a day, the amount of dirt that falls out is amazing. Maybe the old-fashioned ways do work best!)

+ If you have any old candles, artificial flowers or broken ornaments, now is the time to say goodbye to them. Purchase a few new bits and pieces to make your lounge feel fresh and new.

BEDROOMS

+ Change all bedding and put it in the wash.
+ Clean the mattress by giving it a really good vacuum and spray with fabric refresher. Leave the window open for a few hours so it gets a very good airing. If you have any stains use an upholstery cleaner.
+ Turn the mattress before putting clean bedding back on the bed (see also pages 75-76).
+ Move cabinets and dressing tables and thoroughly vacuum underneath them.
+ Clean all the skirting boards.
+ Use a multipurpose spray on furniture, then dry with a buffing cloth and polish or use a glass cleaner.
+ Organise your wardrobes and bedroom drawers (see tip on page 168).
+ Empty out drawers and clean the inside of them. A vacuum nozzle can work really well here. Line underwear drawers with tumble dryer sheets to keep them smelling fresh.

- In children's bedrooms, clean the toys. You can put some plastic toys in the dishwasher; disinfect those you can't with a product spray. Pop soft toys into the washing machine.
- Take down the curtains and wash or dry clean. Alternatively, vacuum them and use a fabric refresher to refresh.

Tip

Wardrobes are another place in the house where you can hide items away. This needs to STOP. Take everything out of the wardrobes and have a good look at the clothes you have. Ask yourself these questions:

- Do I wear it?
- Do I like it?
- Does it still fit?

If you have answered no to any of these questions then it's time for that piece of clothing to GO! Organise a fashion swap shop with friends, have a car boot sale, sell on a web-based selling site or offer items to charity. Someone else will get benefit from your unwanted items so don't just let them hang there. It's time to get them out and make room for new pieces that you actually want to and will wear.

CUPBOARDS

Cupboards are great for storage, but can get over-full. 'Out of sight out of mind' often seems to be the general attitude towards using them. To keep an organised home, we can't do this. If you are a cupboard hoarder, this needs to STOP!

Start by removing everything from the cupboards and sort into piles as you are doing so: e.g. coats, shoes, paperwork, arts and crafts, games, kid's toys, ironing equipment, and so on.

Look at the items and work out whether there are any you do not need or haven't touched in the last 6 months. Either give them to charity, have a car boot sale, or maybe decide to use them.

While the cupboard is empty, get in there with the vacuum, then wash down the walls and the door. Hang up an air freshener to keep it smelling good.

Now, start to put the useful items away. Having a place for everything is key. You will find that having organised cupboards will really help you and will keep your home in a much better order.

Downstairs cupboard
+ Store cleaning items such as the vacuum and ironing board to one side. Make this the cleaning side of your cupboard. To save space, invest in storage hooks and hang up anything that you can.

- If you don't have shelves, add some and then dedicate a shelf to a particular area. You could put children's arts and craft items on one shelf, books on another shelf, family paperwork on another, and so on.
- Add a clothes rail for coats.
- Pop scarves, gloves and hats neatly into a storage box – don't just chuck them in.
- Keep shoes paired together. Use a peg to peg them and line them up neatly or give each family member a dedicated plastic storage tub, so they know where to put their shoes when they come in.

Upstairs cupboard

- Keep towels in an order: guest towels, children's towels, or towels that match particular bathrooms. Don't just chuck them in – fold them all well so they sit straight in the cupboard. Keep separate piles for different sizes: bath sheets, large towels and smaller or hand towels. Keep face flannels in a storage box.
- Bedding should be stored together in sets – this includes fitted sheets, sheets, pillow cases and cushion covers. Don't store pillow cases inside the duvet covers as they will get creased and won't air well.
- Store cleaning products for the upstairs in this cupboard – this will save you from going up and down for products and will ensure that if you see a sudden issue that you need to clean straightaway, you will have the right products to hand.
- Keep your toilet rolls neatly in a box or tub in the cupboard.
- Store spare bathroom toiletries in the upstairs cupboard. This way the bathroom doesn't get overcrowded with unwanted products and you know you have spares for when you run out.

HOME OFFICE/WORK SPACE

+ Take everything off your desk.
+ Sort through paperwork and clutter. If it's not needed, then throw it away – don't hang onto unwanted bits and pieces as they soon mount up. Organise into labelled trays and folders and keep these neatly in a cabinet or on a shelf.
+ Clean your computer keyboard. Turn upside down and shake out any crumbs and use an ear bud to clean the keys and get into the small gaps.
+ Wipe down the computer monitor with a multipurpose spray and a damp cloth.
+ Disinfect the telephone and your computer mouse.
+ Wipe down or vacuum your chair.
+ Wipe any wires where dust can potentially build up.

OUTDOORS

Front/back door

It's so important that the entrance of your home is nice and clean, as this is people's first impression of you. Use a brush to knock off any cobwebs, leaves and debris from the door and porch. Use a bucket of warm soapy water and a sponge to wash everything down, paying attention to the frame, letterbox and window. Rinse clean, ideally with a pressure washer. To ensure it is shining, with no streak marks, buff dry with an old towel. If you have any flower pots, tidy them up to make your front porch more inviting and create a perfect first impression for your guests.

Wheelie bins

I do use a wheelie-bin cleaning service and, if nothing else, it ensures the inside regularly gets a burst of product and water. I clean the lid myself as much as I can – if it's a nice sunny day, I get out there and give it a quick wipe. For a spring clean, get the pressure washer out and giving it a really good blast. Before doing so, spray in a good strong cleaning product to get rid of those ghastly bin smells.

Patio furniture

+ **Plastic and wrought iron** Wipe with a clean cloth dampened with a mixture of water and a mild washing-up liquid. Rinse by hosing down and leave to dry naturally in the sun.

+ **Wicker and teak** Use a soft scrubbing brush dampened with water and a mild oil-based soap (such as Murphy Oil Soap). Rinse by hosing down. For maintenance, hose down every few weeks to prevent dirt build-up in crevices.

+ **Aluminium** To remove scuff marks, use a soft cloth dampened with water and a small amount of washing-up liquid or dish soap (abrasive cleaners and brushes will scratch). Rinse by hosing down.

Garage

+ **Door** You will need a ladder for this job to get right to the top, but be careful – ideally get someone to hold it for you. Before you start, knock off any cobwebs or dry leaves etc. with a brush. With a bucket of warm soapy water (you can use washing-up liquid for this) and a sponge, wet down the door liberally. Thoroughly rinse, ideally with a pressure washer – this will help to remove any stubborn dirt and build-up of cobwebs.

+ **Floor** Choose a dry day and take out everything that is movable. Sweep the floor and give it a good wash using a pressure washer, if you have one.

+ **Organise** Sort through the items before you put them back in, deciding what you do and don't need. Try to keep items in separate sections: bikes, pet care, decorating equipment and materials, gardening equipment, and so on. This way, everything has a designated area and is easier to find.

Spring Cleaning Schedules

Bathrooms

- ☐ Open the window when cleaning with chemicals.
- ☐ Empty bins and then wash them out.
- ☐ Pick up bath mats and remove towels. These are now for the wash.
- ☐ Scrub bath with a multipurpose bathroom cleaner, then fill with warm water and leave a capful of bleach. This can be emptied once the bathroom is finished.
- ☐ Wipe down sinks with a multipurpose cleaner.
- ☐ Scrub the shower tiles, paying attention to the grout as well at the tile. Buff this dry with a glass cleaner for shine.
- ☐ Wash down the shower door; if you have stubborn water marks use some limescale remover and then buff these dry.
- ☐ Soak the shower tray with bleach and put a generous amount down the plughole. Leave to soak before rinsing.
- ☐ Scrub the toilet, clean all around the pan and the bottom. Leave in bleach.
- ☐ Use glass cleaner on the mirrors and the window.
- ☐ Clean out cabinets. Remove any items that are out of date or that you are no longer using and clean the inside thoroughly and then the outside.
- ☐ Wash the floor, steam or get on your hands and knees and get in all the nooks and crannies.
- ☐ Rinse away the bleach that's been soaking.
- ☐ Add in clean towels and bath mats.

Bedrooms

- ☐ Change bedding.
- ☐ Vacuum and lightly steam mattress and headboard.
- ☐ Put any stray clothes away.
- ☐ Vacuum blinds/curtains.
- ☐ Dust furniture.
- ☐ Organise drawers.
- ☐ Throw away, or give to charity, any items that are not needed.
- ☐ Dust light fittings and the tops of picture frames.
- ☐ Vacuum ceilings, removing any cobwebs.
- ☐ Change over diffusers.

Wardrobes or Dressing Rooms

- ☐ Sort clothes into seasons.
- ☐ Turn hangers to face the same way.
- ☐ Make sure folded items are neat and ordered.
- ☐ If you have items you no longer need, get rid of them.
- ☐ Organise and dust shelves.
- ☐ Organise shoes into pairs, ideally keep boxes so these can be stacked neatly.
- ☐ Vacuum.
- ☐ Polish mirrors.

Home Office

- ☐ Dust office desktops.
- ☐ Clean the keyboard and mouse.
- ☐ Check office supplies (i.e. paper, envelopes, pens, stamps, pens).
- ☐ Sort through loose paperwork and file.
- ☐ Organise and dust shelves.

- [ ] Dust window frame.
- [ ] Clean the window.
- [ ] Run a backup on your computer and delete any old files to give you more space.

Hallway

- [ ] Clean walls and inside the door.
- [ ] Dust any shelves/radiator covers etc. Dust picture frames.
- [ ] Shake and vacuum rug.
- [ ] Organise shoes and coats in the cupboard.

Living Room

- [ ] Lightly steam sofas and chairs.
- [ ] Steam rug.
- [ ] Wash and vacuum the floor.
- [ ] Polish furniture.
- [ ] Polish windows/doors/mirrors.
- [ ] Organise any clutter.
- [ ] Dust TV/DVD/BluRay.
- [ ] Wash cushion covers and any blankets.

Dining Room

- [ ] Clean tabletop and legs.
- [ ] Clean chairs and make sure you turn them over and do the feet as well as the legs.
- [ ] Vacuum blinds/curtains.
- [ ] Vacuum and wash the floor.
- [ ] Polish furniture.
- [ ] Dust light fittings.
- [ ] Dust picture frames.
- [ ] Organise any drawers with placemats and cutlery. (Make sure you still have a full set.)

Kitchen

- [ ] Open the window when using chemicals.
- [ ] Remove all items from the surfaces and wipe down.
- [ ] Wipe the fronts of all the doors and the handles.
- [ ] Remove food from cupboards and wipe these over before replacing items.
- [ ] Empty the fridge and throw away any out-of-date food.
- [ ] Clean the inside of the fridge.
- [ ] Clean the microwave.
- [ ] Clean inside drawers and cutlery tray.
- [ ] Organise cloths and tea towels into neat piles within drawers.
- [ ] Sort recipe folder.
- [ ] Wipe down any splashback or tiles.
- [ ] Wipe the cooker splashback and then buff with baby oil for a shine.
- [ ] Wipe down the cooker top.
- [ ] Clean the oven inside and out.
- [ ] Clean the dishwasher; run on a hot cycle and add in a dishwasher cleaner or use lemon.
- [ ] Empty and clean the bin, paying attention to the lid area where food can get stuck.
- [ ] Vacuum and wash the floor.
- [ ] Wash the window and the window seal.
- [ ] Descale the kettle.

Utility Room

- [ ] Run the washing machine on a hot wash with a washing machine cleaner or use white wine vinegar.
- [ ] Empty the bins and clean.
- [ ] Clean out the vents on the tumble drier.
- [ ] Organise cleaning supplies.
- [ ] Wipe down surfaces.
- [ ] Clean inside cupboards.

Clean yourself fit

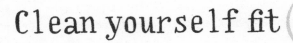

Being a domestic god or goddess can benefit your health as well as your home! Cleaning is one of the best forms of exercise you can do – it's a total body work-out. When you are in the middle of a good clean, you should be working up a good sweat.

MY TOP TIPS:

1   Clean in flexible clothing that allows you to fully move your body.

2   Dance to your favourite play list while you are cleaning.

3   When vacuuming, increase the intensity of the activity by stepping into a lunge. Lunges use most of the major muscles in your lower body, so this is a great action to add to your vacuuming routine!

4   Squat when you are putting things away.

5   Stretch as much as you can when dusting.

6   Try wearing wrist weights to help improve your muscle tone.

7   Make tidying items away a bit harder. Instead of carrying everything up the stairs in one go, split the pile and make a few extra trips or go up and down the stairs as fast as you can!

STATS FOR THE CALORIE COUNTER

How many calories you can burn just by cleaning:

Ironing	around 90 calories per hour
Washing the floors on your hands and knees	187 calories in just 30 minutes
Changing the bedding	100 calories in 30 minutes
Cleaning the bath	90 calories in 15 minutes
Vacuuming	up to 119 calories in 30 minutes (Depending on the size of your home, this can also make a significant dent in your 10,000 recommended steps a day. Try switching from your right hand to your left, and feel the pull in your tummy muscles.)
Cleaning windows	167 calories in 30 minutes
Decluttering the wardrobe	lifting those heavy coats and jumpers can burn around 85 calories in 30 minutes
Moving furniture	100 calories in just 15 minutes
Washing the car	153 calories in just 30 minutes

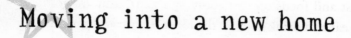

Moving into a new home

Moving into a new home is a very exciting time, but it's so important to give your new home a good clean before you move in, to make it feel like your own. Other people's grime will be polluting the surfaces and door handles and the previous occupant's marks of habitation can make you feel uneasy in your new property. Never fear – a few antibacterial products and a bit of hard work will soon help your home feel brand new and all yours.

Tip

For carpet dents, where furniture has been sitting for years, use ice cubes. Simply lay the ice cubes in the dent and leave to melt. This will bring the pile back on the carpet and the dent will disappear.

- If possible, plan your house move so that you have a day for cleaning before your furniture and furnishings arrive. If you are unable to do this, maybe store as much as you can in the garage or hold on to the moving lorry for an extra day, allowing you more time to clean before your bits and pieces go in.
- Plan the clean: think about the rooms you are going to be using the most and focus on one room at a time. You are going to need to eat and drink and use the toilet, so I would get cracking on the kitchen and bathroom first of all.
- Make sure you are fully armed with cleaning products and tools and gadgets to make the process as smooth as possible.
- Get the whole family involved and ask friends to muck in and support you, too.
- If you can, budget for new flooring – it will benefit you in the long run. Carpets can really hold on to smells and they will never feel like your own. Alternatively, hire or invest in a carpet cleaner. One clean will not be enough – the process will need to be repeated a few times.
- If you are installing new carpets, get the old ones out as soon as possible, along with any lampshades and curtains that will also be holding on to odours from the previous owners.
- Get all those windows opened up as soon as you can, to give the home a really good airing.

STEP-BY-STEP NEW HOME CLEAN

Once the above has been done, it's time to get cracking on the rest of your new home. As always, start at the top and work your way down.

Dust

First, dust the ceilings and remove any cobwebs, concentrating well on the corners. Have a step ladder to hand and go over everywhere with a large feather duster. It will be satisfying to watch the dust drop to the floor. Ceilings do harbour dust, so it's important that you get these clean.

Fixtures and fittings

Door handles, light switches and other buttons all need a really good clean with antibacterial spray. Replace rope light switches, as these can be hard to clean.

As much as I love to use my homemade products in everyday cleaning, when it comes to moving house the bleach does need to come out! Add a good amount of neat bleach to all the sinks and baths and leave to soak to really help kill those germs. After a good soak, scrub clean with an antibacterial spray until they come up like new.

If you have a shower, replace the shower curtain and the shower head as these items harbour a lot of bacteria and germs.

Limescale

If there is limescale on the taps, use a copper cloth to get this off quickly. For the bath or shower tray, apply a good limescale cleaning product and leave it to work or use white wine vinegar. Limescale isn't easy to remove if it has been there a while, so be patient and allow the product time to work. You may find you need to repeat the process, but it's best to get it really clean so the job becomes easy for you in the future.

Toilets

+ If you are keeping the toilets, make sure you replace the seats with new ones.
+ Pour a cheap bottle of cola down each toilet, to ensure the pipes are clean and there are no unwanted blockages that can create nasty smells.
+ Really scrub the toilet bowls clean. You will need to get right down on your hands and knees to get to the back of the toilet and all of the pipes.
+ If the bowl is discoloured, remove as much water as you can by plunging or pumping with a toilet brush or use an old cup to get the water out. Add in neat limescale remover. Do not add any other products, as this is dangerous! Put the seat down and leave overnight. You will wake to find a clean, restored toilet.

Windows

Window frames may need a little TLC, too. Give them a good clean using warm soapy water. For any marks on white PVC frames, use a cream cleaner.

Appliances

If appliances have been left and you are keeping them, ensure you scrub them clean. Invest in a good oven cleaner and pay attention to the hob. You can soak racks, pan supports and burner caps in the bath with water and white wine vinegar to help release the grease.

Tiles

Use a mixture of bicarbonate of soda and white wine vinegar on a little toothbrush to scrub the grout in between the tiles. This will help brings tiles back to life and start to look like new. Clean the tiles and buff dry, then use a glass cleaner to give them the perfect shine.

Sticky marks

If the previous owners had children, you may find sticky hand marks on the walls and pen marks on internal doors or radiators. Don't panic too much, as these marks will come off.

Wall marks A new tennis ball wiped over the mark will help remove it easily, causing no damage to the paintwork. Alternatively, add a tiny drop of fabric conditioner to some warm water and very gently rub the mark away with a microfibre cloth.

Pen and sticker marks Use nail polish remover to wipe sticky marks away with ease. You don't need much and use with care. Afterwards, wipe over with warm soapy water to get rid of the nail polish smell.

Be happy

Be excited about your new home – it will all come together in the end and be the place you always dreamed of!

Tips for new parents

New parents have so much to think about that cleaning really isn't very high on the agenda.

However, it doesn't take long for our homes to become disorganised and for cleaning routines to go out of the window.

Before the pitter-patter of tiny feet, your home may have stayed clean and easy to manage. The kitchen would be fairly quick to wipe down, you could get by with a few loads of laundry a week and just have a big cleaning session on the weekend. Once little ones come along, things change. Babies bring with them a whole bunch of stuff. Who knew that babies could own so many things? The dirty pile of laundry in the corner – it's the baby's. The big pile of clean laundry to fold – it's the baby's. The endless amount of cloths and toys scattered throughout your home; the plastic plates piling up in the sink... you guessed it – they're the baby's.

In the early days of parenthood, it is really easy to blame the lack of cleaning on the baby. The needs of your little one are far more important than a dirty bathroom and unwashed clothes. But you simply can't live like this. Create a good solid routine from day one and, whenever your little one is sleeping, have a quick blitz. Use nap time to sort through the laundry, make yourself some good healthy meals and clean whatever part of the house you can. However, don't forget to add some 'you time' into your baby's nap. Work as a team with your partner and share household chores as well as baby-related tasks.

Top tips for staying organised when time is tight

+ **Structure your day** Write a list of tasks you need to do.
+ **Be organised** Have a place for everything and ensure family members pick up after themselves.
+ **Multi-task** Use time on the phone catching up with a friend to do a little dusting.
+ **Team work** Remember it's not all down to you.
+ **Save time** Keep a few cleaning products in your bathrooms, so you don't have to go back and forth.
+ **Separate laundry** Keep a dedicated laundry basket for the baby next to the changing table.
+ **Do a daily load of washing** Add in an extra spin cycle to allow your washing to dry faster.
+ **Use your cleaning to keep fit** No time for the gym? Set a timer and challenge yourself to do a room in a certain amount of time (see also page 124).
+ **Practical storage** Keep stuffed animals, dummies and rattles in a large, round, flat basket – that way they are on display and easy to find.
+ **Organise baby's clothing drawers by size** Store smallest sizes at the top, getting larger as you go down. As soon as they grow into the next size, remove and immediately store the small clothes in a box (if you want to keep them for another baby) or donate to a friend or charity. Then shift the sizes up a drawer.

HANDY HINT

Use the vacuum from day one, then the baby will be used to the sound and it won't disturb them when they are asleep.

SAFE CLEANING PRODUCTS

Choosing safe cleaning products is a really wise move, particularly if you have babies and young children. My twins were born very prematurely and spent a lot of time in the special care baby unit. Mollie came home on oxygen and they were both very weak. This meant I had to think carefully about what I used around them – I knew that I couldn't expose them to too many harsh chemical-based products. Even though I was in cleaning over-drive, I was very careful about what I used in the home and I always cleaned safely and followed instructions.

When you pop to the supermarket, the choice of cleaning products is huge – there is literally a product for everything. It can make you think that you need them all, but in reality you don't. Some of the products contain a cocktail of harsh chemicals. Using highly toxic products and mixing cleaning products can be so bad for the health of your family and studies have proven that they can actually bring on asthma and allergies. Luckily, more and more ecological products are now on the shelves, which are far less toxic and safer to use around children.

Tip

Don't buy tons of products or be enticed by pretty bottles. Choose a few universal products that will do more than one job.

How to stay safe

✦ Consider using an eco-friendly range.

✦ Try making your own products (see my recipes on pages 15-51), which use ingredients that you probably already have in your kitchen cupboards, such as lemon juice and white wine vinegar.

✦ Always keep windows open when cleaning, so any air-borne toxins can escape and won't stick around in your home.

✦ Make sure you keep your cleaning products out of reach of little ones. Use safety locks if needed.

TOP CLEANING TIPS WHEN YOU HAVE LITTLE ONES

+ Use bibs – even in the very beginning. This way, whenever your baby spits up, you don't have to clean and change an entire outfit each time. Just rinse off or change the bib.
+ Use lemon juice to tackle stains on babies' clothes.
+ Flush stains out from the reverse of bibs and clothes under cold running water.
+ Use a plastic changing mat so you can easily wipe it clean.
+ Use a clean tennis ball to rub away any sticky finger marks that appear on walls.
+ Put plastic toys in the dishwasher with lemon juice to keep them germ-free.
+ Keep towels soft and fluffy for delicate skin by adding a heaped spoonful of bicarbonate of soda to the wash.
+ Use baby oil to shine your stainless steel appliances.
+ Use baby shampoo to clean your make-up brushes.
+ Clean high-chair straps using a toothbrush and toothpaste to bring them back to white. Rinse afterwards with soapy water.
+ Remove mould stains from pushchairs using white wine vinegar.
+ Use a halved onion to help get rid of nasty cooking smells.
+ Rather than harsh carpet cleaner, apply neat vodka to carpet stains and blot using a white cloth.
+ Vacuum the house while carrying your baby in a carrier. Babies love the noise and motion – it is a great way to calm them down (and keep YOU moving, too).

Surviving the festive season

Here's my guide to coping with large family gatherings. I talk about Christmas but you can apply this to any occasion when you are playing host to lots of people.

Christmas can be such an exciting and busy time of the year; it can also be rather overwhelming. Into your already packed daily routine, you now need to insert preparing for Christmas and you often have to deal with a fuller house than usual – be it unexpected guests or a large family gathering. Often, it is difficult to know where to begin. By planning ahead, you'll be able to prepare your home for the festive season and enjoy the holidays with minimal stress.

It's always good to be prepared for Christmas. I advise to start thinking about it as early as September.

MAKE A TO-DO LIST

Make a note of any preparations you will need to make for visiting guests. Establish a timeline for buying presents, shopping for decorations, cooking holiday treats and meals, and decorating the home. Writing down everything you need to do will help guarantee that you get it done. Don't forget to delegate tasks – use other family members and give them a few jobs to do.

Your list might include:

+ Buy presents
+ Write Christmas cards
+ Put up the decorations and tree
+ Prepare guest rooms for friends and family
+ Extra baking (for those mince pie and Christmas puddings)

With Christmas comes extra cleaning tasks, too. When you choose do the big Christmas tidy-up is entirely up to you, but many homeowners prefer to clean over the course of the few days leading up to 25 December. This means they don't feel rushed to get everything done in just one day and they can spend Christmas and Boxing Day relaxing, drinking mulled wine and eating mince pies, without having to worry about chores.

Dividing up the tasks into different areas will make it easier:

DECORATING

Christmas decorations spend most of their time hidden away in cupboards or dusty attics, waiting for their five minutes of fame. But there's no point getting your home spick and span for the festive season only to hang up dirty and dusty decorations. Set aside some time to give the decorations a good clean before hanging them up. A buff with a damp microfibre cloth is a good start and they'll soon look as good as new.

When going through your Christmas decorations, make sure that everything still works. Fairy lights, for example, have a shelf life. If one bulb goes, sometimes the whole set won't work. Test them before you decorate your tree, to see if you need to invest in a new set.

Once you're happy with the decorations, you can focus on the rest of the house.

BATHROOM

Your bathroom will see a lot more traffic as you entertain family and friends over the festive period. One of the most important things you can do during the pre-Christmas clean-up is to get your bathroom as clean and hygienic as possible. Then, try to maintain this level of cleanliness throughout the festive period.

✦ Use a bathroom spray and a toilet cleaning product to ensure that your bathroom is clean and hygienic.
✦ Make sure you have plenty of hand towels and change them daily. Hand towels can harbour lots of germs and, with all those

extra people using them, they won't stay clean for long.

+ Keep the window slightly open, so that fresh air can circulate. It will keep potential mould at bay and eradicate stale smells.

+ To keep your bathroom smelling fresh, add a few drops of your favourite essential oil to the toilet roll tube. It will smell lovely for a couple of days and can be topped up when the fragrance fades.

+ Hang a bundle of eucalyptus in your shower, tied with natural garden twine (this is more moisture-resistant than cotton twine). Hang it on the shower rod, away from the spray of the water. Every time you take a hot shower, you will notice how fresh and clean your bathroom smells.

+ Store a season's worth of toilet paper and other necessities in your guest bathroom, so guests never have to make an awkward request for more.

LIVING ROOM

+ Regular vacuuming is important over the Christmas period.

+ Prior to the big day, get your carpets cleaned before your kids sit on the floor opening and playing with their presents. If you don't have a carpet cleaner, you can hire a professional to do it or hire one from most supermarkets.

+ If you have rugs, flip them over and vacuum the undersides to remove as much dust and dirt as possible.

+ Keep clutter to an absolute minimum. Clear away old newspapers and magazines and make sure anything precious is put away so there are no breakages when you have a full house.

+ Invest in some large throws for the sofas and chairs – this way, sticky fingers and melted chocolate won't ruin your furnishings.

KITCHEN

If you're hosting a big family Christmas dinner, the kitchen really will be the heart of the home. However, the kitchen isn't just for cooking – it's also for safely and hygienically storing food; it's for keeping the glassware, cutlery and crockery clean and shiny; and, if your washing machine is in the kitchen, it's for keeping on top of your laundry. Here are some kitchen tasks you may wish to tackle during the pre-Christmas tidy-up:

+ Clean your oven before Christmas so that it's all ready to cook that turkey to perfection. If your oven is covered in small bits of cremated food, it can affect the taste of the meat, and can also start to smoke, leaving a nasty, lingering smell in the house. Use oven cleaner to get your oven clean again, making sure to follow the directions on the label and taking any necessary safety precautions. Always make sure that the oven is cool before you start to clean it. During the Christmas period, make a point of wiping over the oven after every use with warm soapy water and a good scouring pad. This will make your life easier in the long run.

+ Your work surfaces will be in constant use over Christmas. Ensure you give them a good clean both before the big day and while you're cooking. It's vital to regularly wipe surfaces when preparing food, as uncooked meats can leave germs and bacteria behind.

- We have all got that nice set of cutlery or dinnerware that only makes an appearance on special occasions – now is their time to shine. Set some time aside to clean and polish dinnerware, to make your Christmas meal even more memorable.
- Clean out the fridge, removing any out-of-date food (and recycling the packaging where appropriate). Emptying out the fridge will mean you've got plenty of room for things like wine and trifle! Remove all the shelves and soak them in warm soapy water. If you do have strong-smelling foods, place a little dish of bicarbonate of soda at the back of the fridge to remove odours. Clean the rubber seal with an ear bud and a tiny drop of washing-up liquid, to remove any dirt and crumbs.
- Try to reach the bottom of your laundry basket before the festive period begins in earnest. There is nothing worse than getting ready for a Christmas party and finding that your favourite little black dress or your Christmas jumper is still stuffed in the bottom of the basket waiting for the wash. Having an empty washing basket will give you one less thing to worry about.
- If your glassware has stubborn water stains, gently rub over them with potato skins to remove the grime and rinse as normal. They will come up as good as new.

GUEST BEDROOMS

Even if you're not expecting guests over the festive period, you should always expect the unexpected at Christmas. Whether it's family turning up unannounced, or a friend who pops over and gets talked into opening a bottle of festive bubbly with you and is unable to drive home, you may end up with more guests than you bargained for. This means you should make sure that your guest bedroom is ready to receive people at a moment's notice.

+ Vacuum and polish the guest room to freshen it up. This is particularly important if you don't tend to use the room very often. Rooms that are left unoccupied for long periods can gather dust, making them quite musty.
+ Change the sheets so that they're clean and fresh.
+ Add a few guest towels along with a few basic toiletries to the end of the bed. If someone is staying over when they hadn't planned to, these little touches will be greatly appreciated.
+ You may wish to add a house plant or a room diffuser to the guest room to make it feel more welcoming and 'lived in'. It will make your guests feel more comfortable.
+ Make space in a wardrobe or a set of drawers that your guests can use. If they are planning to stay for a few days, they won't want to be living out of a suitcase. Spray a little air freshener into the wardrobe to keep clothes smelling fresh.
+ You don't want your guests having to stumble around your kitchen in the middle of the night. Before it's time to turn in, fill a pretty carafe with water and set it on a tray, along with a glass, on the bedside table.
+ Write your WIFI password down on a notecard and place it on the bedside table to save guests the trouble of asking for it. If you have one on hand, provide a spare phone charger.

Festive cleaning tips

Declutter

Clutter makes a house look messy, plus it is harder to clean a cluttered room. Grab a washing basket (or three) and clear out everything in your prioritised rooms that doesn't need to be there.

Banish fridge smells

Your fridge will be busier than usual in preparation for your show-stopping Christmas dinner. Place a small plastic tub with some bicarbonate of soda at the back of the middle shelf to keep it odour free. It works as an odour eliminator, all you need is a tiny spoonful of bicarb.

Keep a diffuser to hand

With impending guests and family and friends staying over, bleach the toilet, put in a clean guest towel and keep plenty of spare toilet roll available. Finally, leave a diffuser on a shelf to keep the bathroom smelling good throughout the hectic season.

Get rid of carpet odour

Use a mixture of bicarbonate of soda with a little essential oil to sprinkle over your rugs to keep them smelling fresh. Vacuum up.

Water your Christmas Tree

If you keep your Christmas tree fully hydrated, it will shed fewer needles. Not only does this mean you'll be cleaning up less frequently, it also prevents the needles embedding into the carpet or being transferred throughout the home – causing abrasion and wear and tear to the carpet fibres.

Look after your decorations

If you were faced with broken baubles and tangled tinsel when you opened the decorations box this year, make sure to put them away properly next time. Secure an old pair of tights over your vacuum cleaner and use to gently clean dusty garlands, tinsel and artificial trees. Fragile tree ornaments are best given a light brushing with a soft artist's paintbrush to remove dust.

Stock up on kitchen roll

Christmas is a prime time for spillages. To avoid a big clean up post-Christmas, strategically place kitchen roll around your home, so there's no excuse! People can soak up any spilt bevvies, plus catch any crumbs from those late-night mince pies!

Pick it up

Smashed glasses? Don't panic. Grab a slice of bread and soak up the glass pieces with it. This is one of my favourite party tricks.

Use scent to create a Christmas mood

A harmonious Christmas is on everyone's wish list, which is why calming scents like cinnamon and cloves are so popular at this time of year. Either is great for candles or to use in baking so the delicious smells will waft throughout your home.

A-Z hacks: top cleaning tips of all time

I've mentioned some of these tips already in the book but this A–Z guide should have an answer for every cleaning conundrum that you are likely to come across. These are tried and tested cleaning hacks that actually work!

A

Alka-Seltzer Drop your dull-looking jewellery into a glass of fizzing Alka-Seltzer for a few minutes to bring the sparkle back.

Aluminium foil Scissors get blunt so easily, especially if your children keep using them for their arts and crafts projects, but you don't need to replace them – simply use your scissors to cut up a piece of aluminium foil. It will sharpen them in an instant.

B

Bin smells Place a cotton pad dampened with a few drops of your favourite essential oil into the bottom of your bin to help it stay smelling fresh and clean.

Blinds I never advise using water to clean Venetian blind slats – it can leave horrible dusty water marks. A weekly dry dust is all they should need. The best way to clean these is with tumble dryer sheets – they really lift the dirt and leave a lovely fresh smell behind. Alternatively, an old pair of socks also works.

Broken glass Pick up broken glass that has fallen onto the floor with a slice of bread.

C

Ceilings To clean ceilings, use a flat-headed mop. Hold it up high and move it along the ceilings to keep them dust-free.

Chewing gum If you've ever sat in chewing gum or managed to get it on any of your clothes, you'll know what a pain it is to remove. Simply pop your clothing into the freezer for a few hours – the frozen gum is then really easy to pick off.

Chopping boards Chopping boards can pick up odours from onions, fish and meat that hot soapy water can't always disperse. Rub them with half a lemon and a sprinkle of salt. Leave for a few minutes, then rinse with hot soapy water. The lemon will deodorise and lift any food stains.

Stick to wooden chopping boards rather than plastic. Wood contains several natural substances, such as tannin and vanillin, that discourage the growth of bacteria.

Cleaning cloths and sponges Your sponges and cloths work hard so they will appreciate a quick spa treatment. Blast them in the microwave for a few minutes to kill all the germs or put them in the dishwasher on the top shelf.

Collars and cuffs It's easy for sweat, oil and general grime to stick to shirt collars and cuffs and sometimes a general wash isn't enough to remove it. Just very gently rub some regular hair shampoo into the stains, give them a little scrub, then pop back into the washing machine.

Copper pans Copper is in fashion right now and copper pans are a gorgeous way to modernise your kitchen. If they get dirty after use, there's a cheap solution hiding in your cupboard. Humble tomato ketchup is actually great for cleaning and will make copper pans shine after a quick rub.

~
D

Dents in carpets and rugs Heavy furniture can leave carpets and rugs with dents. Get rid of them by leaving a row of ice cubes inside the dents, then simply allow them to melt into the pile to bring it back to life.

Drains Give your drains a good clear once a month. Throw down some bicarbonate of soda followed by some white wine vinegar and watch it fizz. After 30 minutes, flush with water. If you have a lot of hair or bits of stubborn food stuck in there, use an old mascara brush to get right in and remove it.

Dusting Always start your dusting at the top of the room. Start with the ceiling lights, picture rails and window frames. This way, you drive the dust to the floor where it can be easily vacuumed up.

✦ Dust furniture with a slightly damp cloth. Dry cloths aren't very good at picking up dust and will drag it over the area you are trying to clean.

✦ When dusting wooden furniture, always work in the direction of the grain.

Ẽ
E

Elbow grease Sometimes all we need is good old-fashioned elbow grease for all our household cleaning.

Erasers Use a nail file to remove nasty bits from stationery erasers.

F̃
F

Felt-tip marks If the children have gone crazy with the marker pens on your bannisters, table, or anything else made from wood, rub it gently with a little bit of toothpaste to lift off the stain. Then go and buy them a nice set of pencils instead!

Flowers Make fresh flowers last longer by add a drop of vodka or a 2-pence piece to the water.

Fridge odours Place a small dish of bicarbonate of soda at the back of the fridge to soak up bad smells.

G̃
G

Glasses After washing drinking glasses, dunk them in a bowl of water and white wine vinegar, then drain upside down – this will get rid of the cloudy effect.

Always store drinking glasses upright. If you store them upside down, the air will be trapped and will go stale. At the same time, the rim of your glasses will be in contact with the shelf – if that's not clean, your glasses won't be either.

Gloss kitchen cabinets These can be a pain to keep streak-free with regular cleaning products. Restore their shine by using a small amount of glass cleaner and buff using circular motions.

H̃
H

Hob After cleaning your stainless steel hob, keep it nice and shiny by adding the tiniest drop of baby oil and buff.

~
I

Iron To clean a sticky iron, mix one part salt with one part white vinegar in a microwave-safe bowl. Microwave on high for about 30 seconds, then stir to dissolve the salt. Dip a cloth into the mixture and vigorously rub the bottom of your iron. This should remove the residue that is causing the dragging and give your iron a good clean and shine.

~
J

Petroleum jelly This is great for softening and shining up leather shoes, jackets and furniture – you only need the tiniest amount.

~
K

Kettle Use a mixture of part water and part white wine vinegar or lemon juice to keep limescale and hard water stains away (see page 27).

~
L

Lampshades Use a lint roller to take the dust off lampshades. A lint roller is delicate and won't push the shade out of shape like a vacuum nozzle could.

~
M

Microwave Microwaves can easily be splattered with food and, if you forget to clean up straight away, this will harden and become hard to wipe clean. Place a bowl of water with a few slices of lemon in the microwave and set on high for 5 minutes. The steam will soften the dirt and the lemons will degrease and make it smell amazing.

Moths Clothes moths can be such a pain, especially through the summer months. Once you have got them, they can be tricky to remove. Make a natural repellent by bagging up some dried herbs, including lavender, cloves, bay, rosemary or thyme, in some fabric bags. Hang them in your wardrobe and place in your drawers.

~

N

Net curtains Nets will need an occasional wash to restore the colour and quality of the material. Wash in the washing machine on a cool delicate cycle with detergent and a large spoonful of white wine vinegar, then hang them back up to dry.

~

O

Onions Onions absorb odours so, for a natural deodoriser, leave out half an onion for a few hours to absorb cooking, musty or paint smells.

~

P

Pans and dishes If you have cooked- or dried-on food stuck to your pots and dishes, save the elbow grease for other jobs, fill the kitchen sink with hot water, add a dishwasher tablet and leave to soak. Afterwards, the grease and grime should just slide away.

Pet hair Use a wet rubber glove to collect up hair easily.

~

Q

Quick cleaning Follow my '5-minute Challenge' to bash out your daily cleaning effectively (see pages 124-127).

~
R

Rugs and carpets Sprinkle bicarbonate of soda mixed with your favourite essential oil over high-traffic areas or areas where pets settle. Use a sieve to keep it even, leave it on for a few hours (maybe even overnight) and then vacuum away. The bicarb will soak up any odours.

Rust patches If you have a few rust patches on your towel rails or radiators or on garden furniture, dab on some ketchup before rubbing away with a cloth – the rust will lift right off.

Rusty cutlery If your knives and forks have rusted, stick their ends into an onion a couple of times and the rust should lift straight off.

~
S

Smelly shoes Trainers can be the worst offenders, but there are a few ways to keep them smelling fresh. Add in tea bags, then leave under the radiator when not in use; sprinkle with bicarb and tip out before you wear them next; or spray in a squirt of dry shampoo after wearing.

Smoothie maker/blender After you have made your drink or blended your soup, act quickly to avoid stains. Add a squirt of washing-up liquid and a little warm water, then put the cup or bowl back onto the unit with the lid firmly on. Blitz, then just give it a quick rinse.

Squeaky wooden floors Use talcum or baby powder to silence noisy wooden floors. Sprinkle some onto the floor, then sweep into the cracks, wiping away the excess.

Stainless steel After cleaning your stainless steel use a tiny drop of baby oil and buff with a clean microfibre cloth for the ultimate shine.

Sticker stains If your children have gone sticker happy and plastered them all over their bedrooms door don't panic. Use a tiny amount of nail polish remover and gently rub over the mark.

Sticky scissors Use a cotton wool pad and nail varnish remover to clean sticky Sellotape glue off scissors.

~
T

Toaster crumbs Get tricky-to-reach crumbs and burnt bits out of your toaster by unplugging it and sweeping with a pastry brush. This will help your toaster last longer, as well as making crumbs less likely to catch and burn.

Toilet limescale Limescale build-up in the toilet can be unsightly and bleach will only mask the problem for a few days. Bring a grubby-looking toilet back to sparkling white by pouring in a can of cola. Let it sit in the bowl overnight, then give it a quick scrub with a brush and flush the next morning for a great effect.

Toothbrushes Don't throw away your old toothbrush – it can be a really useful tool. Give it a rinse in boiling water to get rid of any germs, then use it to get into nooks and crannies that your vacuum cleaner can't reach. It's especially handy in the bathroom, for cleaning hard-to-reach areas around the tap or drain.

Towels When washing towels, omit the fabric conditioner. Fabric conditioner can damage fibres and make them feel stiff.

TV remote controls TV remotes are one of the germiest items in your home – they collect all types of bacteria on a daily basis. Try cleaning them with a small amount of hand sanitiser and a paper towel. For extra effectiveness, use a cotton bud to get those hard-to-reach areas between the buttons.

Ũ
U

Urine stains on mattresses If you have small children, they often have the odd accident. Mix a solution of bicarbonate of soda, white wine vinegar and water together and spray onto the stain. Scrub it in, leave for 15 minutes, then blot dry. You can also use shaving foam in exactly the same way!

Umbrella The next time you climb up to clean your chandelier or light fitting, take your umbrella with you. Open it and hook the handle to the fixture so it hangs upside down. It will catch the dust as it falls.

Ṽ
V

Vacuuming delicate areas Pull a pair of tights over the nozzle of your vacuum cleaner – it works really well for vacuuming dust off artificial flowers or ornaments and other items of value.

W̃
W

Wall marks Remove marks on painted walls by running a new tennis ball over them.

Water marks For water marks on draining boards and shower screens, cut a lemon in half, cover it in bicarbonate of soda and then rub it over the marks. Leave for 15 minutes, then rinse.

Windows Always wash windows on a cloudy day. The sun will dry cleaning products far too quickly and will encourage those unsightly streaks.

X̃
X

X-ray vision Sometimes you feel you need this to see right into those hard-to-reach areas. Have a small torch to hand and shine it into crevices so you can see any potential dust and dirt you may have missed.

Ỹ

Yellowing pillows To prevent yellow staining on pillows, I always advise using pillow protectors. If your pillows are already yellowing, you can buy whitening agents to go in the washing machine. Alternatively, add a big spoonful of bicarbonate of soda along with a good biological washing powder (not liquid or tablets) to the wash. Finally, partly tumble-dry the pillows. Remove them while still damp and leave them to dry outdoors in direct sunlight for as long as possible, turning so that both sides catch the sun. They will come up white and smell wonderfully fresh.

Z̃

Zones Break down your cleaning regime into zones and tackle one area at a time. By tackling them little and often, you can keep on top of cleaning tasks.

Index

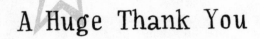

A Huge Thank You

Firstly I would like to thank the fabulous people at both Harper*Collins* and PFD for giving me this amazing opportunity and making my dream come true.

A massive thank you also to my wonderful little family who have supported me on this journey and who gave the belief that I could actually write a book. They all have to put up with me insta-storying most of our lives and take daily photographs for me so I can share all my wonderful cleaning tips and home hacks.

Also to the wonderful people at Betty TV who took a chance on me and gave me a regular slot on Channel 4's *Obsessive Compulsive Cleaners*.

And lastly, to all of my wonderful followers who have stuck with me for the past two years and have held me up with such amazing support and encouragement, even when I felt like giving up.